Jerusalem, Judea and Samaria

cover photo *View of Jerusalem
from the Mount of Olives*
frontispiece *Autumn in the
Mountains of Efraim*

WEIDENFELD COLOUR GUIDES TO ISRAEL

General Editor: Rinna Samuel

JERUSALEM
JUDEA AND SAMARIA

Sylvia Mann
Photography by David Harris

Weidenfeld and Nicolson Jerusalem
together with Steimatzky's Agency

Weidenfeld and Nicolson Jerusalem
19 Herzog Street
Jerusalem

Weidenfeld and Nicolson
11 St John's Hill
London SW 11

Designed by Alex Berlyne

ISBN 0297 76629 5

Composed by Keter Press, Jerusalem and printed by
Japhet Press, Tel Aviv, 1973

Contents

Editor's Foreword

Although this guide to Jerusalem, Judea and Samaria speaks for itself, there are a few things to be said about it – and about the three books which are its companion volumes – that may help you both to enjoy and to use it as fully as possible.

To begin with, this is the first time that a set of regional guides to Israel and the territories under Israeli administration since 1967 has been published. Each of the four Weidenfeld Guides has been written by a different author and is illustrated by a different photographer; each book is a distinct entity unto itself, but all four books together make up a series. Published simultaneously with this book are the Weidenfeld Guide to Tel Aviv and Environs, the Weidenfeld Guide to Galilee and Golan and the Weidenfeld Guide to the Negev and Sinai.

Secondly, these books have been conceived as guides in the broadest rather than the narrowest sense of the word and have been written in the hope that they will be read with equal pleasure and profit by tourists visiting the country, by people planning a trip to it and even by sedentary voyagers, travel-book buffs.

Thirdly, another feature of the Weidenfeld Guides is that they are in no way intended to substitute for the kind of last-minute, very detailed information which can and should be obtained from Israel Tourist Information Offices and/or reliable travel agencies. You will not learn in these pages how or where to rent a car in Israel, what visas you do or do not need, the latest rate of exchange for foreign currency or how and where you can send a cable at night. But you will, we think, learn a great deal about the various parts of the country; what is worth visiting extensively; what can be seen in a few minutes or skipped altogether; and what traces the long past has left on the fascinating present.

Finally, each book has been written very much with its own special territory in mind: Tel Aviv is the heart of Israel's cultural, literary, artistic and theatrical life, so Mendel Kohansky's book concentrates on these aspects; Jerusalem can only be seen properly if you actually walk its streets, guidebook in hand, and Sylvia Mann, therefore, has concentrated on the historical and archaeological information about one of the world's most fabulous cities and its environs; the north of Israel is tailor-made for drives and walks, the ideal place for sightseeing combined with relaxing, so Hadassah Bat Haim takes you on a leisurely journey that starts on the way to Haifa and reaches the Golan Heights. The Weidenfeld Guide to the Negev and Sinai is the only such book available for tourists travelling through the Negev to Eilat and Sinai. It lingers particularly over Beersheba, Massada, Ein Gedi, the Dead Sea and covers the entire Sinai Peninsula (including St Katherine's Monastery) and all of the Gaza Strip.

Since the Six Day War of 1967, the total area under Israeli administration – of course, including Israel itself – extends from the Golan Heights in the north to Sharm el-Sheikh in the south, bounded in the north by Lebanon and Syria, in the east by the Jordan River and in the south-west by the Gulf of Suez and the Suez Canal – all told 89,359 square kilometres of which 20,700 square kilometres are Israel proper, or Israel as it was before June 1967.

Israel's population includes approximately three million Jews (some 18% of world Jewry), about half of whom came to the Jewish State from some seventy-one countries of the Diaspora, and roughly 250,000 Arabs, of whom the vast majority are Moslems. The total population of the areas administered by Israel since 1967 (the so-called West Bank, i.e., the entire area west of the Jordan River, the Gaza Strip, the Sinai Peninsula and the Golan Heights) consists of close to a million Arabs, some 600,000 of whom live in Judea and Samaria and about 337,000 of whom live in the Gaza Strip.

Any capsule geography of the State of Israel must stress the fact that the climate varies immensely from region to region, from the Sahara-like heat and aridity of large stretches of the Negev and Sinai to north Mediterranean temperate weather in most of the Galilee; from the Riviera-like warm summers and balmy winters on the coastal plain to the fairly cool summers and crisp, cold winters of Jerusalem. On the whole, Israel is hot and relatively dry in the summer; rainy but not very cold (by European or American standards) in the winter. Since climate and clothing are intimately related, this is the place to deal quickly with the question of what to wear. The answer is very simple: in the summer, as little as possible, though a sweater is useful in Jerusalem, parts of Galilee and Sinai at night; in the winter, since many homes in Israel are not yet centrally heated and it can be chilly, warm clothes are necessary. Incidentally, all mythology to the contrary notwithstanding, women do dress up for parties or 'gala' events in Israel.

Getting from one place to another can be done in several ways: inland flights, rented cars (with or without guides), taxis, the railway – which runs from Tel Aviv to as far north as Nahariya, to Jerusalem and as far south as Dimona – and buses. You can travel all over Israel either by ordinary buses or on specially organized guided tours in air-conditioned buses.

Things to bear in mind include the fact that banks, government institutions, shops, offices, movies and theatres (except in purely Arab areas such as the Old City of Jerusalem) close early on Friday afternoons and remain closed all day Saturday, though places of entertainment usually open up again after dark on Saturday. Moslem and Christian establishments are closed on Fridays and Sundays, respectively. Information about hotels, restaurants, tours and so forth (including bookings and recommendations) can be obtained from the Tourist Information Offices in all large Israeli towns and cities and, of course, in most foreign capitals.

With this, let me wish you an interesting, good and not too tiring time in Israel. Believe me, getting behind your own or somebody else's steering wheel and seeing the country for yourself is much better than another thousand words from me.

Rehovot

Rinna Samuel

Milestones

A brief chronology of what happened, when and to whom, in the course of Israel's roughly 4,000-year-long history

The period generally referred to as the biblical era begins about **1700 BC,** when Abraham came to the country, and ends about **AD 73** with the last stand of the Jews against the Romans at Massada. Within this span, the important landmarks are:

The Exodus from Egypt in the **13th century BC**

The return of the Children of Israel to the Promised Land sometime between the **12th and the 11th centuries BC**

King David makes Jerusalem his capital about **1000 BC**

King Solomon builds the Temple in Jerusalem about **950**

Israel is conquered by the Assyrians in **721 BC** and Judah by the Babylonians in **586 BC,** at which time Jerusalem is sacked and the First Temple destroyed.

The Jews return from the Babylonian captivity in **538 BC** and by **515 BC** they have rebuilt the Temple.

Alexander the Great conquers Palestine in **333**

The uprising of the Maccabees (known also as the Hasmoneans) takes place about **168 BC**; a century later, in **63 BC**, the Roman rule over the country begins.

The wars of the Jews against the Romans start in **AD 66.** The Second Temple is destroyed by Titus in **AD 70** and in **AD 73** Massada falls.

From **AD 132 to 135** Jewish rebels, under Bar-Kokhba's leadership, rise against Rome, but their rebellion is suppressed.

From approximately **AD 395 to AD 636** Palestine is under the sway of the Eastern (Byzantine) part of the Roman Empire.

In **AD 636** the country is conquered by the Arabs, who hold it until about **1072,** when the Seljuk Turks take over.

In **1100,** the Crusaders capture Jerusalem and establish their Latin Kingdom, but in **1187** Saladin recaptures the city for the Moslems and in **1291** Crusader rule come to an end.

In **1517** Ottoman Turks conquer the Arab Empire and Palestine becomes part of the Turkish Empire. In **1799** Napoleon Bonaparte invades Egypt and Palestine but his campaign fails.

In **1870** (the date traditionally marking the beginning of the Jewish reclamation of Palestine) a Jewish agricultural school is established outside Jaffa, and in **1878** Petach Tikvah, the first modern Jewish village in Palestine, is founded. In **1882** the first fairly large-scale Jewish immigration (*aliya*) to Palestine gets underway; Theodor Herzl's book *The Jewish State* is published in **1895;** the first Zionist Congress takes place in Switzerland in **1897;** and both the first all-Jewish city of Tel Aviv and Palestine's first collective settlement, Degania, are founded in **1909.**

1917 sees the signing of the Balfour Declaration (in which the British Government ambiguously informs the Zionists that it will favour the 'establishment of a Jewish National Home' in the Holy Land) and the beginning of the successful Allied military campaign to deliver the Middle East from the Turks, which leads, in **1922,** among other things, to the League of Nations giving the Mandate over Palestine to Great Britain.

In **1947,** following the refusal of the Jewish population to accept British restrictions on Jewish immigration and land purchase in Palestine before, during and after the European Holocaust, the U.N. General Assembly resolves to partition the country into a Jewish and an Arab State.

On **14 May 1948** the State of Israel is born, and five Arab armies invade the country.

Israel's War of Independence lasts until the spring of **1949;** in the autumn of that year the new state's Jewish population reaches its first million and by **November 1950** the 500,000th new immigrant will have entered Israel.

The pace of Jewish immigration to Israel continues throughout the **early 1950s,** as does open Arab hostility against – and armed infiltration into – the Jewish State.

In **October 1956,** following an Egyptian-Czech arms agreement, Israel moves against Egyptian troop concentrations in Sinai and the Gaza Strip, evacuating these territories in **March 1957,** when the U.N., guaranteeing Israel free passage in the Tiran Straits, stations troops of the U.N. Emergency Force on the southern borders.

During the **first half of the 1960's**, Israel receives its millionth new immigrant, inaugurates two large new towns (Arad in the Negev and Karmiel in the north), builds the port of Ashdod and establishes diplomatic relations with West Germany. Shmuel Yosef Agnon is awarded the Nobel Prize for Literature, and the Israel Museum opens in Jerusalem.

In **May 1967** the state celebrates its nineteenth birthday, and a few days later the U.N. Emergency Force is withdrawn from Sinai and the Gaza Strip at the demand of the Egyptians; Egyptian President Nasser closes the Tiran Straits to Israeli shipping; and Jordan and Iraq join Egypt and Syria in creating a united Arab command and proclaiming war on Israel.

On **5 June 1967** Egyptian armoured columns begin to move towards Israel and Jordan and Syria join the attack. In a massive six-day counter-move, Israel destroys the enemy airpower, takes the Gaza Strip and the entire Sinai Peninsula, forces the Jordanian Arab Legion to evacuate Jerusalem and the areas west of the Jordan River and smashes Syrian positions on the Golan Heights, thus establishing new cease-fire lines and unifying Jerusalem.

In the **autumn of 1968** the Egyptians begin the so-called War of Attrition across the Suez Canal, and the Arab campaign of terror is launched with the attack on an El Al plane in Athens.

By **1970** Golda Meir has become Israel's fourth Prime Minister, the War of Attrition has come to an end and Israel has welcomed its three millionth citizen.

Preface

This book is intended to give a general, overall picture of both Old and New Jerusalem, reunited after the Six Day War of June 1967; of the western sections which were part of Israel since the creation of the State in May 1948; and of the administered territories – Samaria to the north, Jericho and the Dead Sea to the east, and Bethlehem and Hebron to the south.

Each district has its own special character; each its own special beauty; each its own special problems. Although the total area covered is barely 120 kilometres from north to south, and 50 from west to east, and the distances between places is short, each has its specific history, much of it stemming directly from the Bible.

The hub of this section of the country is the Old City of Jerusalem, its 4 kilometres of medieval walls enclosing a magical panorama of scenes and people: stepped narrow lanes thronged with jostling crowds; goods brought from all corners of the Arab world; donkeys nimbly trotting over the cobblestones; and orthodox Jews rubbing shoulders with bearded priests and brown-habited Franciscan monks weave an unforgettable tapestry.

New Jerusalem, developing over the past century, made tremendous strides during the nineteen years it was cut off from its mother city, but none as great as those made after the Six Day War. Swift changes took place: public services were merged, the police force integrated and skilled Arab workers lent a hand in rebuilding and expanding the city. Today, broad shrub-lined highways, modern housing estates and educational institutions, skyscrapers, monuments and parks, interspersed with mosques, churches and ancient tombs, fill it with interest for visitors from far and near.

Judea and Samaria, taken as an administrative unit after the Six Day War, is more popularly known as the West Bank. This was the name given by the Jordanians to the area west of the Jordan River seized by them in 1948. It includes most of Judea

A Jerusalem street scene

The Judean Desert as seen from Jerusalem

and Samaria and spreads across the range of Hebron-Judean-Samarian hills from south of Hebron to north of Jenin, extends east to the Jordan River and has a population of around 600,000.

The hill road from Jenin to Hebron and Beersheba was a link in the Patriarchs' Way – the age-old highway connecting the northern empires to Egypt and the south – and is generously marked with biblical figures and happenings. Eastward lie the Judean Desert, Jericho and the Dead Sea, where Joshua and the Children of Israel, the Hasmoneans and Herodians, New Testament personalities and the early monastic orders played out their roles against the dramatic background of the lowest place on earth.

This book takes you through some of the towns and byways of Jerusalem and the West Bank, tells you something of its rich past and dynamic present and helps you get to know the Jews, Christians and Moslems who together make up the population of the Holy Land.

A Nutshell History of Jerusalem

Jerusalem is a unique city. Woven into the pattern of human history for nearly five thousand years, the background for most of the Old and New Testaments, the cradle of Christianity and one of the three holiest towns in Moslem ideology, Jerusalem combines the fascination of the past with the vigour and amenities of the 20th century.

From time immemorial a special light has illuminated Jerusalem, gilding its shadowed stones; glowing through its green western valleys and blazing down upon the desert stretching eastwards to the Dead Sea some 1,200 metres below. Sometimes this light has burned dimly and the city has slumbered, but mostly it has focussed sharply upon the stage setting of Jerusalem, with its walls and towers, its motley throngs, its temples and its palaces.

Many fateful scenes of tremendous significance to all mankind have been enacted on this majestic stage: Abraham's meeting with the Canaanite king Melchizedek, 4,000 years ago; David's conquest of the Jebusite stronghold; the construction of the Temple; the rise of the Hasmonean and Herodian dynasties; Jesus' teaching, his trial and crucifixion; the Roman destruction of the city in AD 70 ; the Crusader Kingdom of Jerusalem; and the latter-day miracles of a resurgent Jewish nation in the 1948 War of Independence and the Six Day War of 1967.

Part of Jerusalem's importance stems from its geographical position. It is located upon Israel's rocky spine, which runs north to south between and parallel to the coastal plain and the Jordan Valley and forms the watershed separating the Mediterranean and the Dead Sea. To the west are fertile valleys capable of providing fruit and grain, while in the east the rain-depleted slopes of the Judean Hills still grow sufficient pasture for rearing sheep and goats.

Along this range, comprising the Samarian and Judean mountains, runs the Patriarchs' Way (Derech Ha'avot), the route trodden by Abraham when he left his home in Ur of the Chaldees and journeyed southwards through Shechem, Jerusalem, Bethlehem and Hebron to Egypt. Jerusalem stands about 800 metres above sea level – lower than the Hebron Hills to the south or those of Bethel to the north – hollowing a pass through the mountains and linking the cultures of the Mediterranean with those of the mysterious East.

These north–south, west–east caravan trails brought with them not only trade and merchandise, but merchants and travellers with sharp eyes and knowledgeable minds who made Jerusalem the cross-roads of the world.

Jerusalem itself is situated on a triangular, south-pointing plateau, with Mount Moriah – the Temple Mount – forming its open northern border. On the south, separated from each other by the Tyropoeon ('Cheesemakers') Valley, are two smaller hills: Mount Zion, bordered by the Hinnom Valley on the west, and narrow Mount Ophel, edged by the Valley of Kidron on the east. It was on Mount Ophel that Canaanite, or Jebusite, Jerusalem stood, where 4,000 years back Abraham was welcomed by 'Melchizedek king of Salem [who] brought forth bread and wine: and he was the priest of the most high God'. Strange it is that even in those far-off days, Jerusalem was already a holy city, for of all the Canaanite city-states, only the kings of Jerusalem added *zedek* (holy) to their names.

Eight centuries later David captured the fortified town – also called the stronghold of Zion – and lived there peaceably with the Jebusite inhabitants. From Arauneh the Jebusite he 'bought the threshing floor . . . for fifty shekels of silver. And built there an altar unto the Lord'. Above it Solomon erected the First Temple, turning Jerusalem into the place of pilgrimage it has remained ever since. After Solomon's death, the monarchy was split into two – Israel in the north, and Judah in the south, with Jerusalem as its capital and Solomon's son, Rehoboam, as its king.

Israel fell to the Assyrians in 722 BC, and Judah to Babylonian forces in 586 BC, when Nebuchadnezzar, ruler of Babylon, sacked Jerusalem. The First Temple was burned and looted, and many of the golden utensils and other precious objects stolen, while Jerusalem's inhabitants were either killed or carried off to the land of their captors. Fifty years later, when Cyrus, king of Persia, invaded Babylon, he encouraged the Jews to return to their homeland, even declaring that 'the Lord God of heaven hath charged me to build him a house in Jerusalem, which is in Judah.' Under the leadership of Ezra, then of Nehemiah, Jerusalem and the Temple were rebuilt, and Jerusalem was strengthened by an influx of Jews from the rest of the country. Nehemiah tells how they 'cast lots to bring one of ten to dwell in Jerusalem'.

Around 332 BC, when the Persian Empire fell to young Alexander of Macedon, Judah, too, came into the Greek political sphere. Alexander's brilliant career was cut short by his early death in 323 BC, and his generals battled for the control of his realm. As a result, the province of Judah was among the lands taken by Ptolemy, whose headquarters were at Alexandria in Egypt, while another general, Seleucus, made his capital at Antioch in Syria. Jerusalem remained under the rule of the Ptolemies for more than a century, when it was captured by the Syrian Seleucids.

Greek influence was at first benevolent, but when religious practices were interfered with, rebellion stirred. In 163 BC the Temple was reconsecrated by the family of the Maccabees, or Hasmoneans, who established a great empire extending across the Jordan River. Following Hasmonean rule, Herod the Great, founder of the Herodian dynasty, was a shrewd politician who managed to hold on to a fair amount of independence, although nominally a vassal of Rome. He expanded the empire of the Hasmoneans, rebuilt Jerusalem and the Temple and created new towns throughout Palestine.

In AD 70 the Roman legions destroyed the Second Temple and the city. The Jewish population suffered severely, until in AD 132 they revolted under the banner of Shimon Bar Kokhba and regained Jerusalem; but three years later, Hadrian demolished it and built over its ruins the square Roman townlet of Aelia Capitolina.

Grey twilight enshrouded Judah's ancient capital. Even its name was forgotten until Byzantine Empress Helena, mother of Constantine, converted to Christianity and in AD 326 made a pilgrimage to the Holy Land, where, encouraged by her son, she set up shrines marking the birth, activities and death of Jesus.

During the Persian invasion of AD 614 almost all of the

Model of Jerusalem during Second Temple period, Holyland Hotel

churches were burned and looted and Christians were massacred without mercy. The Persians remained in power for some thirteen years. Then Byzantine Emperor Heraclius recaptured Jerusalem, but his triumph was short-lived, for scarcely a decade later came the Moslem conquest, fired by a new religion – Islam – and a new prophet – Mohammed. On Mount Moriah, site of Solomon's Temple, the Moslems erected the Dome of the Rock. Jerusalem, claimed by Islam to be its third most important city, actually became an insignificant townlet in a vast Arab empire.

Four centuries of peaceable Moslem rule was shattered in 1009 by mad Caliph Mansur el-Hakim, and again, ninety years later by the Crusaders. Hakim was a strange young man who, although his mother was a Russian Christian and two of his uncles were high-ranking church officials in Alexandria and Jerusalem, was violently anti-Christian. He was only twenty-four when he made his savage attack on the Church of the Holy Sepulchre, following it with equally savage restrictions on Christians and Jews. Ten years after he declared that he was an incarnation of God, and was held to be so by a new sect, the Druze, some of whom live in Israel and have become part of its loyal population.

Compared with the Crusaders, however, Hakim was a mere amateur in the art of cruelty. On 14 July 1099, they broke through the defences of Jerusalem, burned the Jewish community in their synagogue and slaughtered every Moslem – man, woman and child. The Crusader Kingdom of Jerusalem lasted until 1187, when Saladin regained the city, soon taken over by the Mamelukes.

With the beginning of Turkish sovereignty in 1517, Suleiman the Magnificent rebuilt Jerusalem's ramparts, aqueducts and cisterns, and put up a series of beautiful *sebils,* or fountains, for travellers and pilgrims. This burst of energy over, the town faced 450 years of neglect and apathy, lightened only by increasing Jewish interest in the Holy City. Families fleeing Spain's religious persecution reinforced Jerusalem's small Jewish population, and they were joined by immigrants from Eastern Europe. Towards the end of the 19th century,

Dr Theodore Herzl's vision of a Jewish State gained momentum and became one of the most constructive movements of modern times.

World War One hastened the disintegration of the Ottoman Empire, and in December 1917 British General Edmund Allenby entered Jerusalem on foot, starting off the thirty-year British Mandate over Palestine. Although the Mandate undertook to set up a National Home for the Jews, little was done, and increasing antagonism between the Jews and Arabs, and between both and the British, flared into open warfare – and the War of Independence of 1948.

The State of Israel – the first independent Jewish State for nearly two thousand years – was declared on 14 May 1948. British forces withdrew, but fighting between Jews and Arabs intensified and thousands of lives were lost. The Old City was besieged and fell to the Jordanians, while New Jerusalem, with less than 100,000 Jewish inhabitants, became the capital of Israel.

Tackled capably and well, the reborn City of Zion took upon itself tasks which might have daunted the best-established municipality. Mass immigration had to be dealt with, alongside health, housing, education and a multitude of other problems. Within a short time Jerusalem became a word of praise, while Jews everywhere turned to it as a symbol of their age-old covenant with God – a beacon of light and constancy in an indifferent world.

Yet Jerusalem was incomplete. Approachable only from the west, it was located at the end of a *cul-de-sac* known as the Jerusalem Corridor. Its connection with the north, east and south were blocked, and its heart – the Old City, enclosing Mount Moriah and the Western Wall – was in Jordanian hands.

The Six Day War flung wide the gates of Jerusalem. Every barrier was swept aside; roads were opened to all points of the compass; Jews were reunited with their ancient shrines, and nearly 100,000 Arabs joined their 200,000 Jewish fellow-citizens to begin a fuller, happier episode in the eternal drama of Jerusalem.

Sha'ar Hagai

The Road to Jerusalem

Most visitors to Israel arrive by air at Lod Airport and make the ascent to Jerusalem along the ancient hill road from the coast. Travelling between broad fields and young forests, your mind goes back to the many battles fought over this strategic mountain pass from the Mediterranean – the Great Sea of the ancients – to Jerusalem, none of which was more decisive than those of April 1948.

The fate of Jerusalem hung in the balance. Supplies were of paramount importance if it were to hold out, but the Arab Legion had control of the road, and only by a superhuman effort, entailing heavy loss of life and of transport, was the city stocked up before the siege. At Sha'ar Hagai (Arabic: *Bab el-Wad*; the 'Gate of the Valley') you can still see the wrecks of the vehicles burnt out while trying to reach beleaguered Jerusalem. After hostilities ceased, the stretch be-

The Trappist Monastery at Latrun

tween Sha'albim and Latrun was cut off by the Arabs, so a loop road was quickly built and was used until June 1967 saw the highway reopened – the highway you are driving along today.

As the road leaves the plain and begins its gentle climb into the Judean Hills, your attention is caught by the Monastery of Latrun, its Italian-style architecture blending with the dark-green pines and luscious vineyards. Founded fifty years ago, it is the home of Trappist monks who have taken vows of silence, although one is always assigned to act as host and to sell the honey, cheese and wine which they prepare.

Close by is the traditional site of Emmaus, where Judah the Maccabee defeated the Greek forces of Antiochus IV, and where the New Testament story places the resurrected Jesus' meeting with two of his disciples. Marked by the ruins of a 3rd-century AD church – the earliest yet discovered in the country – often called the Church of the Maccabees, it is overlooked by the Crusader castle of Les Toron des Chevaliers, guarding the Valley of Ayalon leading up to Jerusalem.

The 'Latrun Road' through the Valley of Ayalon

Not every Christian denomination believes this to be the true Emmaus, and a little to the north-west is a second one, at the Arab village of Qubeibe (see page 209). Here the Franciscans have built a church incorporating the foundations of the house where Cleophas and Simon asked Jesus to 'Abide with us, for it is toward evening and the day is far spent.'

Past Latrun, at the Sha'ar Hagai junction, stands a rambling Turkish Khan, once the 'Half-way House' between Jerusalem and Jaffa; and opposite, behind the filling station, is a small Turkish guard tower, the last of a series protecting 19th-century travellers. Cedars, fir and pine trees clothe the slopes, reaching the spectacular Martyrs' Forest and Memorial Cave honouring victims of the Holocaust.

A livelier aspect of the highway is reflected in two open-air swimming pools and recreation centres – one at Shoresh and the other at Ma'ale Hahamisha, both with comfortable guest houses, while at Ein Hemed (also called Aqua Bella, or Beautiful Water) is a picturesque picnic spot. Here, around the remains of a Crusader convent, a natural spring has been channelled among green lawns and ancient conduits, creating a pleasant park for an afternoon's relaxation.

Turning off the new Abu Ghosh bypass some 12 kilometres before Jerusalem, you find yourself in the village where, in Joshua's days, lived the Gibeonites, who were to be 'hewers of wood and drawers of water for the house of God'. Its Moslem Arab inhabitants are mostly descendants of the 18th-century chief (Arabic: *mukhtar*) Aissa Mohammed Abu Ghosh, who increased his family fortunes by imposing an illegal toll on everyone journeying to Jerusalem.

The Arabs of Abu Ghosh, about 2,000 in number, are typical of the 300 million Moslems scattered throughout the world. Their religion is Islam, founded by Mohammed in AD 622, the year of the *Hegira*, or Flight, signifying the flight of Mohammed from Mecca to Medina after he denounced the old gods.

Islam is a monotheistic religion, with Allah as its deity, Mohammed as its prophet and the Koran its divine book. It broke with Judaism and Christianity by taking Friday as its day of rest, yet it reveres many biblical figures and holds strictly to the injunction forbidding graven images. Moslems are not permitted to drink wine or indulge in gambling, and they are expected to pray five times daily after washing their hands and feet. The direction of prayer is towards Mecca. Mohammed himself returned to Mecca in 630, broke the idols (except for the great black stone called the Kabah) and declared it a city of pilgrimage. Moslems are encouraged to make this pilgrimage (*hadj*) at least once, preferably with a group, and then may wear special headgear showing they have been to Mecca.

Moslems have a special calendar, its year 1 being AD 622, when Mohammed fled from Mecca. Each year comprises 345 days made up of twelve lunar months, and their principal festivals are *Ramadan*, the 9th Moslem month, with fasting from sunrise to sunset; *Id el-Fitr*, three days of feasting at the end of the Ramadan fast; and *Id el-Adha*, the festival of sacrifice commemorating the ransom of Abraham's son Ishmael with a ram. The first ten days of the month of *Muharram* are days of mourning for the prophet's murdered grandson, Husain.

An aspect of special interest about Abu Ghosh is the fact that its inhabitants put up no resistance against the Israeli forces during the 1948 War of Independence. On the con-

The Crusader church in Abu Ghosh

trary, the villagers readily accepted the new régime and were quickly integrated into the Jewish State. Within the village itself, the Crusader church is well worth seeing. Now a monastery, the solid, rectangular structure was taken over and repaired by the French Benedictine Order about a hundred years ago. In the crypt – a baptistry during Crusader times – bubbles a rich spring, which the Romans used to fill a large open reservoir.

Beside the church entrance lies a stone sarcophagus of some unnamed medieval warrior and also a Roman milestone. Set into the wall is a tablet recording the presence of the Tenth Roman Legion, while on the grounds are the remnants of a 9th-century Arab khan used by the Crusaders.

Above Abu Ghosh is biblical Kiryat Yearim, the resting-place of the Holy Ark, captured in battle by the Philistines and brought by the 'men of Kiryat Yearim . . . into the house of Abinadab in the Hill'. Here it remained for twenty years, until 'David brought it, with dance and song, into Jerusalem'.

Today, the Convent of the Ark of the Covenant and a modern church built on Byzantine foundations stand where Abinadab's house once stood. A towering figure of the Madonna and Child, visible from far off, rises from the roof, and within the church are 1,500-year-old tessellated pavements, as well as a mosaic floor said to date back to Maccabean days. Pillars and decorated stone fragments can be seen in abundance, and a second Latin-lettered tablet recalls Rome's Tenth Legion.

Two kilometres further down the road, strategic Mount Castel towers 750 metres above sea level. Once an important Roman fort (Latin: *castellum*) guarding the highway, it was also a Crusader strongpoint and much, much later, the site of an Arab village. From the village attacks could easily be made upon vehicles travelling up to Jerusalem from the coast, and just before the outbreak of the 1948 war, this is exactly what happened. Jewish forces stormed the hill, and in the battle that followed the Arab commander of Jerusalem, Abdul Khader Husseini, was killed. His troops panicked and fled, and Mount Castel was taken.

Motza, on the western outskirts of the capital, mingles old and new. Upper Motza boasts growing numbers of comfortable homes with colourful gardens, as well as the Arza convalescent home named for the tree planted there by Theodor Herzl in 1898. In Lower Motza, founded as early as 1860, is a spacious synagogue built by the first group of Jews who settled here. Abandoned for a time after the riots of 1929, when Arabs ran amok in the village, it has now been repaired and is fulfilling its original purpose.

Rome ruled this part of the world for centuries. Roman soldiers came, married local wives, and on demobilization were encouraged by the authorities to settle, forming colonies loyal to the powers-that-be. One of these colonies was at Motza, and the nearby abandoned hamlet of Kolonia carries an echo down two thousand years of history.

An almond tree in blossom near the Hadassah Medical Centre

Dinosaur prints at Beit Zayit

On the hill above is Mevaseret Zion – an immigrant absorption centre mainly for those from western countries. Geared to make the always-difficult process of acclimatization easier, the immigrants are provided with housing for the first few months, with facilities for learning Hebrew, and with help in finding jobs or retraining where necessary.

Almost immediately, a clearly marked path leads to the thriving *moshav* (cooperative village) of Beit Zayit, where one of the world's rarities can be found. On a rock clearing near the central silo, protected for ages by layers of grey shale, are the fossilized footprints of a family of dinosaurs. Estimated to have been implanted here, on the muddy banks of a widespread, shallow lagoon a hundred million years before, the markings show all sizes of three-toed, bird-like dinosaur feet. More than a hundred prints were discovered, in addition to trails made by their tails while steadying these somewhat awkward reptiles.

A concert in progress at Binyanei Ha'uma

The Entrance to Jerusalem

Travelling up between a double avenue of olive trees, you reach Jerusalem proper. Here is the busy Egged terminal for inter-urban buses and the looming bulk of the Convention Centre, popularly called Binyanei Ha'uma ('Buildings of the Nation'). Symbolic of New Jerusalem, it serves as the concert hall for the renowned Israel Philharmonic Orchestra; as an auditorium for drama, choirs and ballet; and as an exhibition compound and for mass meetings and ceremonies.

You have had a foretaste of Jerusalem's varied charms while driving up to the capital. Having arrived, take a closer look at this strange, unrelated conglomeration of people and neighbourhoods, each of which grew up with its own special characteristics. Some are Sephardi Jews, whose origin is in the Spanish-speaking or Oriental countries; others are East

European Ashkenazi Jews, although marriage between the two groups is now so frequent that the resulting Israeli-born offspring are called *sabras* – after the sweet prickly pear growing by the wayside. The fanatically orthodox folk of Mea She'arim and Geula, where Yiddish is the spoken language and the round felt hat and black caftan the accepted dress, are poles apart from their neighbours in the English-speaking American Colony, and both are completely different from the down-to-earth Kurds and Moroccans of Mahane Yehuda.

An interesting glimpse into the habits and customs of various ethnic groups – like the Yemenite, Persian and Bukharian Jews – is given by the Friday afternoon lecture and synagogue tour. The tour usually starts at 2 p.m. from Egged Tours on Jaffa Road and from United Tours in the King David Hotel Annex, but it is best to check with your hotel desk.

Variations between the communities and districts are great. Higher housing and educational standards in, for example, Beit Hakerem and Talbieh, with their comfortable homes and well-tended gardens, are bound to create living patterns other than those in the Gonen area or Nahalat Ahim, while within the Old City walls the diversity is even more marked. Moslem Arabs, Christian Arabs, Armenians, Copts and Ethiopians form closed communities, often using their own language and clinging to their own dress and customs.

Various Christian sects, too, provide additional colour to the kaleidoscope of Jerusalem's citizens, and it is easy to distinguish the Franciscan monks dressed in loose brown robes, the spotless gowns of the White Fathers and the sweeping black cloaks and silver ornaments of the Greek and Russian church dignitaries.

Your best plan is to settle down in the hotel of your choice – which must be booked well in advance – and begin to map out a programme of sightseeing for the Old City, Jerusalem and its surroundings and Judea and Samaria. If you have neglected to reserve a room, the Government Tourist Infor-

The interior of the Italian Synagogue in Jerusalem

y Memorial. below 'The Monster'

mation Office at 24 King George Avenue (telephone 227281/2), or the one inside the Jaffa Gate (telephone 82295/6) will be glad to help.

Jerusalem has a wide variety of hotels geared to every taste and pocket. In the luxury class is the King David in West Jerusalem and the Intercontinental, with a breathtaking view over the Old City, in East Jerusalem. First-class hotels include the Diplomat, President, Kings, Moriah, Shalom, and the Holyland (in West Jerusalem), and Mount Scopus, the National Palace, St George and the American Colony – see p. 56 – (in East Jerusalem).

– see p. 56 –

You need have no hesitation in booking a room in Jerusalem for the whole of your stay in the region covered by Jerusalem, Judea and Samaria. Even the farthest point mentioned – Jenin – is barely 80 kilometres away, while most of the places of outstanding interest are much nearer.

A satisfactory starting point is the 1:50-scale miniature model of Herodian Jerusalem set in the garden of the Holyland Hotel. An extraordinary piece of work, it was financed and initiated by the late Mr H. Kroch, hotel owner and philanthropist, and supervised by Professor M. Avi-Yonah, who based his design on Mishnaic and other authenticated records.

Precise in every detail, the model covers about one dunam (quarter of an acre) and is most delicately constructed of minute stone blocks, with every building, every pillar, capital, well, cistern and pool clearly shown. You can see in it the magnificent Second Temple in all its glory of gold and carvings, Herod's palace with its three gorgeous towers and the earlier Palace of the Hasmonean kings. You can see the Western Wall, the Temple courts, the Gates of Hulda, and innumerable other points which will make your later visit to the Old City far more meaningful.

While in this vicinity, drive out to the wooded hills around Khirbet Sa'adim, where the Kennedy Memorial in the form of a sturdy tree cut down in its prime recalls the life and violent death of John F. Kennedy.

Not far away is the Hadassah-Hebrew University Medical Centre, sponsored by Hadassah, the Women's Zionist Organization of America. The Centre includes an eight-hundred-bed

hospital; an out-patien
Jews and Arabs daily; a
ing and pharmacy, as
Treatment and Resear
the Medical Centre
dazzling series of twe
twelve sons of Jacob.

Hadassah has been
since 1961, but its hum
educator Henrietta Sz
women to provide me
nurses and dentists we
tals and infant-care sta
ing and vocational tra

In 1939 a three-hun
Mount Scopus in coo
years afterwards seve
on their way to the h
services transferred t
new complex built he
is rising on its previou

above The Kenne

Hadassah's pionee
too, became one of i
School for Girls was
Centre teaching fine
Israel Education Ser
education, providir
matriculation stud
student counselling

Ein Karem, wit
Testament 'villag
Baptist was bor
Temple priests,
years', became
site of the aged
the Nativity of
A small mosq
the Italian Chu
elderly cousin,

above *The Chagall Windows.* below *View of Ein Karem*

Crusader church is skilfully integrated into the present one, and the entrance court, protected by wrought-iron gates, is lined with ceramic plaques bearing the Magnificat prayer in many languages. A blue-and-gold mosaic pediment pictures Mary's journey from Nazareth.

The architect of the Church of the Visitation was Antonio Barluzzi, who died in 1960. An Italian expert in church architecture, he specialized in incorporating older structures into his designs and in creating an atmosphere of love and reverence in all his buildings. Israel is fortunate in possessing many fine examples of Barluzzi's work.

Crowding above Ein Karem are essential but unattractive low-cost housing units – some monsters eight floors high, some one- or two-storey homes. Since 1954 thousands of immigrants and evacuated families have been settled in Kiryat Hayovel, then in Ir Ganim and Kiryat Menahem. These are typically fight-against-time buildings of the early years of mass immigration, when Jerusalem absorbed almost 100,000 newcomers under difficult conditions.

Mount Herzl, or the Hill of Remembrance, is the highest point in western Jerusalem, being 830 metres above sea level. On its summit is the grave of Theodor Herzl – journalist, visionary and the propagator of political Zionism – and those of Ze'ev and Joanna Jabotinsky and of other Zionist leaders.

Dr Herzl's study, with many of his private papers, has been transferred here as part of a museum, and the documents shed a sombre light on this outstanding personality. Unhappy in his private life, Herzl lived apart from his wife and children and died in 1904 at the early age of forty-four. His will requested that he be buried near his parents until 'the Jewish people will transfer my remains to Palestine'. Forty-five years later, the re-interment was carried out by a Jewish government in the independent State of Israel.

Part of Mount Herzl is taken up by the beautifully landscaped Military Cemetery, where the victims of Israel's all-too-frequent wars are buried. Those who fell during World War Two, in the War of Independence of 1948, in the defence of the Old City, during the 1956 Sinai Campaign and in the Six

above *The Chagall Windows.* below *View of Ein Karem*

Crusader church is skilfully integrated into the present one, and the entrance court, protected by wrought-iron gates, is lined with ceramic plaques bearing the Magnificat prayer in many languages. A blue-and-gold mosaic pediment pictures Mary's journey from Nazareth.

The architect of the Church of the Visitation was Antonio Barluzzi, who died in 1960. An Italian expert in church architecture, he specialized in incorporating older structures into his designs and in creating an atmosphere of love and reverence in all his buildings. Israel is fortunate in possessing many fine examples of Barluzzi's work.

Crowding above Ein Karem are essential but unattractive low-cost housing units – some monsters eight floors high, some one- or two-storey homes. Since 1954 thousands of immigrants and evacuated families have been settled in Kiryat Hayovel, then in Ir Ganim and Kiryat Menahem. These are typically fight-against-time buildings of the early years of mass immigration, when Jerusalem absorbed almost 100,000 newcomers under difficult conditions.

Mount Herzl, or the Hill of Remembrance, is the highest point in western Jerusalem, being 830 metres above sea level. On its summit is the grave of Theodor Herzl – journalist, visionary and the propagator of political Zionism – and those of Ze'ev and Joanna Jabotinsky and of other Zionist leaders.

Dr Herzl's study, with many of his private papers, has been transferred here as part of a museum, and the documents shed a sombre light on this outstanding personality. Unhappy in his private life, Herzl lived apart from his wife and children and died in 1904 at the early age of forty-four. His will requested that he be buried near his parents until 'the Jewish people will transfer my remains to Palestine'. Forty-five years later, the re-interment was carried out by a Jewish government in the independent State of Israel.

Part of Mount Herzl is taken up by the beautifully landscaped Military Cemetery, where the victims of Israel's all-too-frequent wars are buried. Those who fell during World War Two, in the War of Independence of 1948, in the defence of the Old City, during the 1956 Sinai Campaign and in the Six

hospital; an out-patients' clinic serving more than a thousand Jews and Arabs daily; and schools of medicine, dentistry, nursing and pharmacy, as well as a soon-to-be-completed Cancer Treatment and Research Institute. Hadassah's special pride is the Medical Centre Synagogue, adorned by Marc Chagall's dazzling series of twelve stained-glass windows depicting the twelve sons of Jacob.

Hadassah has been based here, on the fringe of Ein Karem, only since 1961, but its humane work started in 1912, when teacher and educator Henrietta Szold called together a committee of twelve women to provide medical aid for Palestine. A team of physicians, nurses and dentists were soon on their way, and badly needed hospitals and infant-care stations were established, while schools for nursing and vocational training were set up.

In 1939 a three-hundred-bed Medical Centre was constructed on Mount Scopus in cooperation with the Hebrew University, but nine years afterwards seventy-eight of its staff were ambushed and killed on their way to the hospital. It was then left under police guard; the services transferred to makeshift premises in town; and eventually a new complex built here, in Ein Karem. Today a second Medical Centre is rising on its previous site on Mount Scopus.

Hadassah's pioneering was not limited to medical work. Education, too, became one of its major projects, and in 1942 the Alice Seligsberg School for Girls was opened, to be followed by the Louis D. Brandeis Centre teaching fine mechanics, printing and electronics. Hadassah's Israel Education Services expanded in 1970 into the field of higher education, providing two years of specialized training for post-matriculation students. The Vocational Guidance Institute does student counselling and carries out research in this subject.

Ein Karem, with its spires and minarets, is said to be the New Testament 'village in the hill country of Judah' where John the Baptist was born. The story tells how Zechariah, one of the Temple priests, and his wife Elizabeth, both 'well stricken in years', became the parents of an only son. On the traditional site of the aged couple's home stands the Spanish Church of the Nativity of St John.

A small mosque marks the Spring of Mary on the path up to the Italian Church of the Visitation, where Mary visited her elderly cousin, Elisabeth, during her pregnancy. Part of the

above The Kennedy Memorial. below 'The Monster'

mation Office at 24 King George Avenue (telephone 227281/2), or the one inside the Jaffa Gate (telephone 82295/6) will be glad to help.

Jerusalem has a wide variety of hotels geared to every taste and pocket. In the luxury class is the King David in West Jerusalem and the Intercontinental, with a breathtaking view over the Old City, in East Jerusalem. First-class hotels include the Diplomat, President, Kings, Moriah, Shalom, and the Holyland (in West Jerusalem), and Mount Scopus, the National Palace, St George and the American Colony – see p. 56 – (in East Jerusalem).

You need have no hesitation in booking a room in Jerusalem for the whole of your stay in the region covered by Jerusalem, Judea and Samaria. Even the farthest point mentioned – Jenin – is barely 80 kilometres away, while most of the places of outstanding interest are much nearer.

A satisfactory starting point is the 1:50-scale miniature model of Herodian Jerusalem set in the garden of the Holyland Hotel. An extraordinary piece of work, it was financed and initiated by the late Mr H. Kroch, hotel owner and philanthropist, and supervised by Professor M. Avi-Yonah, who based his design on Mishnaic and other authenticated records.

Precise in every detail, the model covers about one dunam (quarter of an acre) and is most delicately constructed of minute stone blocks, with every building, every pillar, capital, well, cistern and pool clearly shown. You can see in it the magnificent Second Temple in all its glory of gold and carvings, Herod's palace with its three gorgeous towers and the earlier Palace of the Hasmonean kings. You can see the Western Wall, the Temple courts, the Gates of Hulda, and innumerable other points which will make your later visit to the Old City far more meaningful.

While in this vicinity, drive out to the wooded hills around Khirbet Sa'adim, where the Kennedy Memorial in the form of a sturdy tree cut down in its prime recalls the life and violent death of John F. Kennedy.

Not far away is the Hadassah-Hebrew University Medical Centre, sponsored by Hadassah, the Women's Zionist Organization of America. The Centre includes an eight-hundred-bed

Yad Vashem

Day War – they lie at rest, their marble-pillowed graves strewn with rosemary.

On another spur of the mountain is Yad Vashem, a monument to the six million Jews systematically stamped out barely a generation ago. The Hebrew words mean hand (or memorial) and name and are taken from the book of Isaiah 56:5, where the prophet says that the Lord will give to every unfortunate 'in mine house and within my temple walls a place and . . . an everlasting name that shall not be cut off'.

Marked from afar by a soaring metal pillar recently erected, the Yad Vashem compound is approached by the Avenue of the Righteous Gentiles, where every tree and sapling commemorates or has been planted by a community or an individual who extended a hand to help his Jewish brother. These lights among the shadows flickered in many lands, including Germany itself.

The administration building contains a reference library of thousands of books, a reading room and the archives of the Holocaust on microfilm – newspapers, diaries and drawings of concentration camp prisoners, lists of those who vanished and those who escaped and every detail of the legal proceedings against Nazi criminals.

Outside the offices, a broad stairway ascends to the massive Memorial Shrine built of water-smoothed Galilean boulders topped by plain grey concrete. David Palombo's forceful metal gates open into a dim hall, its sunken floor tiled with grey-black mosaics. A ramp joins the entrance to the exit gates designed by Bezalel Schatz, while a cone of sunlight filters through the highest point in the tent-like roof on to an eternal flame burning above a casket of human ashes from the cremation ovens.

Set out in approximate geographic arrangement are twenty-two ceramic floor panels, each bearing the name of a concentration camp. Auschwitz, Bergen-Belsen, Buchenwald, Dachau, Theresienstadt and the others – although some twenty-five years have passed since their dissolution – still strike terror in every heart.

One of the ways in which Israel commemorates the six million victims of the Holocaust is by a mass rally on the patio adjoining the Memorial Shrine on the anniversary of the fall of the Warsaw Ghetto. The tragedy of the Warsaw Ghetto began in 1940, when the Nazis walled around some 400,000 Jews, caging them in so that they were at the mercy of their oppressors. Within two years over 300,000 souls had been deported to the so-called work camps – and were never heard of again.

Soon realizing that their compatriots had been carried off not to work camps but to death camps, the remnant of the Warsaw Ghetto started an active revolt against the Nazis. Armed with any weapon which came to hand – out-dated rifles, iron bars, even bottles – the Jews managed to put up a remarkable fight. However, they could not withstand the might of the German Army, and eventually, house by house, trench by trench, the defenders of the Warsaw Ghetto were hounded to their death. On 8 May 1943 (27th of Nissan according to the Hebrew calendar) the ghetto fell. The Nazis set the compound ablaze, and the most heroic symbol of Polish Jewry was no more.

A drive of some 5 kilometres along Herzl Boulevard will quickly transport you back to the bus terminal, and from there you continue on to Jerusalem's northern suburbs. Mea

A courtyard in Mea She'arim

She'arim ('District of a Hundred Gates') is probably the best known. Inhabited almost entirely by East European Ashkenazi Jews who hold to their 17th-century dress, customs and speech, it consists of a series of courtyards, each with a single gate for safety, and windows facing into the yard. Visitors are asked not to offend the local people, and notices are displayed everywhere requesting that they 'dress modestly, with head covered!'

Founded in 1874, Mea She'arim was one of the earliest settlements outside the Old City walls. Conditions were dan-

Hassidim in Jerusalem

gerous and times were hard, so almost every courtyard was 'adopted' by some European community, who would support it with funds and sometimes send members to join the group. Synagogues and *yeshivot* (Talmudic academies) abound, and this preoccupation with the minutae of religious dogma, the use of Yiddish in daily life, the peculiarity of dress and the almost universal beard and sidelocks worn by the men have given Mea She'arim a special place in the mosaic that is Jerusalem.

Mea She'arim's ultra-orthodox Jews reflect but one aspect of Judaism, although their single-mindedness and attachment to their particular spiritual leader make them an influential factor in the life of the country. Generally speaking, Judaism is the original monotheistic faith formulated well over three thousand years ago, when Moses brought the Tablets of the Law from Mount Sinai to the Children of Israel, who were assembled at its foot.

Based on the Pentateuch – the first five books of the Bible – the Jewish faith is founded on certain well-defined precepts of daily living and the worship of God. Saturday, the seventh day of the week, is its day of rest; it has strict rules of conduct and dietary laws (which are scrupulously followed by government institutions, at public functions, in the Armed Services, in hospitals and schools, and by a large portion of Israel's Jews).

The Jewish calendar starts from the Creation, and the year is divided into twelve months of twenty-eight days, catching up with the regular calendar by adding an extra month every four years. Each day begins on the previous evening, so that sundown on Friday is already the Sabbath, which in turn finishes at sundown on Saturday.

Since the fall of the Second Temple, a central place of gathering has no special significance. Prayers, customarily chanted three times daily while facing the Temple Mount, may be said alone, or preferably with a group of ten males above the age of thirteen (a *minyan*). The concept of a synagogue is more that of a Beit Haknesset (Meeting House) where people gather to worship, study and discuss.

The custom of circumcising all males at the age of eight days dates back to Genesis, when God told Abraham 'Every man child among you shall be circumcised . . . and it shall be a token of the covenant betwixt me and you'. Widely practised, too, is the *bar mitzvah* ceremony on a boy's thirteenth birthday, when he becomes a full member of the community. Less observed are the precepts of binding on *tephillin* – small leather cubes containing portions of the Law – and the wearing of the fringed undergarment (*tzitzioth*). Adult Jews wrap themselves in a fringed prayer shawl (*tallit*) when praying in a synagogue, while the skull cap is a reminder that God is above.

Marriage in Israel is under the jurisdiction of the Rabbinical courts. The ceremony is carried out beneath a canopy – often out of doors – during which the marriage contract (*ketuba*) is read and a plain gold ring placed on the bride's finger, while at the end of the ceremony the groom breaks a glass in memory of the Temple's destruction.

The Jews have always been attached to their land, and their festivals are both national and agricultural ones, beginning with the three Pilgrim Festivals when the people used to stream into Jerusalem for prayer and thanksgiving. On Passover, the week-long feast of unleavened bread, preceded by the Seder service, joy at the Exodus from Egypt combines with that of the spring sowing, while on *Pentecost* or the Feast of Weeks (*Shavuoth*) rejoicing at the giving of the Law coincides with the happiness of the first fruits harvest. Tabernacles (*Sukkot*) is a reminder of the wanderings of the Children of Israel in the desert, as well as the festive harvest season. The final days of the week of Tabernacles is *Simhat Torah* (the Rejoicing of the Law).

Days of reckoning were the New Year (*Rosh Hashana*) followed ten days later by the fast of the Day of Atonement (*Yom Kippur*), probably the most generally kept of the Jewish Holy Days. Minor festivals are those of *Purim,* recalling 5th-century BC Queen Esther, who saved her people from persecution, and the Feast of Lights (*Hanukkah*), celebrating the re-consecration of the Temple by the Maccabees in 164 BC. A brand-new springtime holiday, dating from 1948, is Israel's Independence Day, fêted on the 5th day of the Jewish month of *Iyar.*

The woodland housing the Biblical Zoo, where there is a collection of creatures mentioned in the Bible, might well be on another planet instead of a stone's throw away. Peacocks, baboons, bears, deer, lions and a host of other beasts and birds provide a diverting interlude in the day's strenuous sightseeing.

The Biblical Zoo

Nearby Sanhedria is best known for its rock-hewn Second Temple necropolis. One of the family vaults, which has a finely carved pediment above the entrance, comprises about seventy graves dug on three levels and is thought to be the Tomb of the Sanhedrin, the seventy-one-member Jewish parliament of those days. Other beautifully made sepulchres there include the two-thousand-year-old Tomb of the Pillars, with a sunken forecourt and stone benches cut in the solid rock. Twenty-one tombs have already been excavated, and who knows how many more are still hidden under the accumulated soil?

Not far from residential Sanhedria, just north of the main Tel Aviv–Jerusalem highway as it enters the capital, is the industrial zone of Romema, where many light industries such as machine shops, knitting mills, electronic and other small factories and printing presses provide sources of employment. A second industrialized area is Givat Shaul, south of the highway, where there are somewhat heavier undertakings, including one manufacturing electrical equipment and another turning out aluminium products, as well as the central bakeries, flour mills and furniture factories.

A third, more recently established, lies south of the pleasant wooded suburb of Talpiot, from 1948 to 1967 on the edge of Israel's one-time border. The Six Day War gave a great impetus to the development of this whole vicinity, and now garages, workshops, and a large number of small factories, some employing Arab women, have opened up along the broad new road to Bethlehem. A good point about Jerusalem's industries is that they are mainly concentrated into these three places and appear to use smokeless fuel, for there are practically no tall chimneys and no air pollution.

Close to Talpiot is a section known as Katamon, with clusters of beautiful stone houses built in the early decades of this century. With the mass immigration of 1949 and 1950, these houses were utilized for new immigrants and for relocating people living under difficult conditions, while quickly erected apartments were put up on empty spaces all around. These groups of buildings were called lettered

Ramat Eshkol

sections of Katamon, collectively the district of Gonen.
Together with Jerusalem's other southern suburbs of
Kiryat Hayovel, Ir Ganim and Kiryat Menachem, Gonen
absorbed the bulk of the housing problem of that critical
period in the same way as Ramat Eshkol (the 'Heights of
Eshkol', named in honour of Prime Minister Levi Eshkol)
has absorbed much of Jerusalem's population explosion in
the wake of the Six Day War. This time, however, building
standards are higher and economic conditions better, while
a curious aftermath of June 1967 has been the welcome
availability of skilled Arab roadbuilders, masons, smiths and
other craftsmen.

Ramot Eshkol, the French Hill (named for the French
convent built on its summit) and Givat Hamivtar (the 'Divided Hill', from the road running through it) are providing
space for thousands of stone-built homes in an area which
was formerly wasteland. On the highest point of Givat
Hamivtar, a hillock riddled with underground sentry-posts
has been transformed into a memorial park, in the hope that it
will commemorate the last blood spilt in Jerusalem – 'City
of Peace'.

Downtown West Jerusalem

The Heart of the City

The heart of New Jerusalem contains most of the popular
hotels – the King David (with Herod's Family Tomb adjoining),
the Moriah, the President, the Tirat Bat Sheva and the Kings' –
as well as the YMCA hostel directly opposite the King David.
This is an important shopping section, too, with tourist and
travel agencies and stores geared to tourist gifts, both modest
and luxurious, and to collector's items of ritual objects in gold
and silver and rare antiques.

Jerusalem's main commercial centre, however, is that
bounded by Jaffa Road, Ben Yehuda Street and King George
Avenue, where you push your way through good-humoured,
window-shopping throngs. Small as it is, 'The Triangle' – with
the Hamashbir Hamercazi department store on one of its
corners – is the most popular centre for Israelis and visitors
alike. Prices are reasonable; displays show attractive clothing,
leather and silverware, groceries, fruit and wine, as well as
gift shops to supply all needs. Cheerful cafés abound, and it

is a pleasure to rest for a while with a cup of hot coffee and a fresh cheese cake.

In King George Avenue is Hechal Shlomo, the seat of the Chief Rabbinate. The tall, white cut-stone building, donated by Sir Isaac Wolfson and named for his father, also includes a library and reading room, a museum of Judaica, an auditorium, a room housing an interesting series of models depicting biblical events and a synagogue. During the High Holy Days, when the congregation grows, services are held in the entrance hall – which, fortunately, has a gallery for women.

Adjoining is the Jewish Agency complex, with the offices and archives of the World Zionist Organization, the Weizmann Room, the Keren Kayemet and the Keren Hayesod (funds for land reclamation and colonization), as well as the Golden Book records, arranged around a courtyard. Close by is the large Yeshurun Synagogue, while in Hillel Street, across the main road, is the tiny Italian Synagogue, transferred from a small town near Venice where no Jews remained.

Further down, near the King David Hotel, is the modern Hebrew Union College, a department of the Hebrew Union College of Cincinnatti, Ohio. It has a well-equipped auditorium and acts as a centre for archaeological projects, as well as for the Reform Movement in Israel.

Edging on to the Old City are the Mamilla Pool and the Russian Compound. Mamilla Pool, set in a wooded Arab cemetery, is a rectangular masonry-lined open cistern for rain catchment. Built in Herodian days, when the city expanded and extra water was needed for its growing population, this large reservoir has been kept more or less in good shape ever since, for it was an important factor in Jerusalem's water supply. An overflow conduit channelling any surplus water under the Old City ramparts and into the Pool of the Patriarch in the Christian Quarter was open until 1948.

The Russian Compound, barely 500 metres from the Old City walls, is located on a slight rise, where legends tell that

The entrance hall of Hechal Shlomo

46

The Russian Compound

the Assyrian Army camped while preparing to attack Jerusalem in 700 BC and from where Titus planned his successful campaign to overthrow Herod's thriving capital. Rather more than a hundred years ago, in 1860, the Russian Government obtained the land from the Turks to provide facilities for the thousands of Russian pilgrims who came from so far to celebrate Christmas in Jerusalem, often staying on until after the Easter rites in springtime. During the early days of the 20th century their numbers rose to twenty thousand annually!

For them the Czarist Government erected the lofty green-roofed cathedral; built a large structure with a coaching courtyard (now the Israel Police Headquarters) and put up a hospital and separate hostels for men and women. With the outbreak of World War One and the subsequent victory of the Red Army, the torrent of pilgrims ceased, and the Russian Compound lay empty and neglected.

Soon the buildings, except for the cathedral and a few others,

Russian Compound exhibit. overleaf *View from the Mount of Olives*

were taken over to fulfil different functions. One of the hostels still houses a handful of aged Russian nuns, and another, which was a prison under British rule, is now a museum called the Hall of Heroism. Here you can see the cells and gallows for political prisoners, as well as photographs and records of many young Jews who suffered imprisonment and sometimes even death for their ideals.

What was once the residence of the Russian representative now holds an Exhibition of Agricultural Implements in its courtyard. Ancient ploughshares, millstones, olive presses and water wheels explain how Israel's natural products were grown and utilized. Before leaving the compound, note the Russian pilgrim emblem which appears everywhere – on the gatepost, over the doors, on window openings and roads – 'For Zion's sake will I not hold my peace, and for Jerusalem's sake I will not rest' (Isaiah 62:1). Another piquant detail is a half-quarried stone pillar of the measurements of those in Herod's Temple. While being dug out in 20 BC, it apparently cracked and was abandoned.

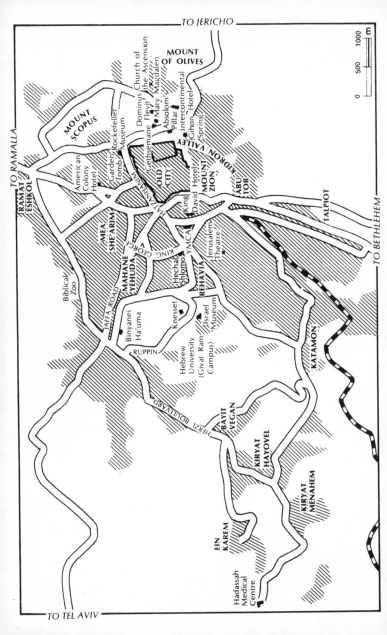

Across the Green Line

Close to the Russian Compound but across the former Green Line – the 1948–67 border separating Israel from Jordan – are a series of Christian pilgrim sites, notably the Chapel of Polyeuctus, the Garden Tomb and St Stephen's Church honouring the first Christian martyr.

When foundations for a house were dug in the Street of the Prophets in 1894, a complete 8 by 5 metre mosaic floor was uncovered above a crypt filled with skeletons. The design pictures a growing vine with tendrils describing multiple circles, each enclosing another variety of bird, while across one end an Armenian inscription proclaims that the chapel – the chapel of St Polyeuctus – was erected 'to the memory and salvation of the souls of all Armenians whose names are known to God alone'.

This lovely 5th-century pavement is the first Grave of the Unknown Soldier, which took the form of a commemorative chapel for the Armenian fighters killed in battle with the Persians in BC 451 and brought here for burial.

The Garden Tomb – a Second Temple mausoleum – is a favourite shrine for Protestant pilgrims, many of whom believe this, rather than the generally accepted Holy Sepulchre, to be the authentic grave of Jesus. This supposition was voiced in 1842 by pilgrim-traveller Otto Thenius, then forty years later it received strong support from British General Charles Gordon, hero of the British action at Khartoum, who was spending a year in Jerusalem to study the Bible.

The cause was energetically taken up in London, an organization was formed and by 1892 sufficient money was collected to landscape the site and have it cared for by a resident warden. Today a tranquil garden laid out with pools, flowerbeds and winding paths, it combines with the ancient cisterns and wine presses to make a fitting background to the rock-cut grave said to be that of Joseph of Arimathea, who took Jesus' body and 'laid it in his own new tomb, which he had hewn out in the rock'.

Adjoining the Garden Tomb is the Grotto of Jeremiah,

The Garden Tomb

traditionally also the Place of Stoning, where executions were carried out. Here, the story goes, St Stephen met his death, and in his memory the Byzantine empress Eudocia erected the Basilica of St Stephen. Today a new church, with much of the original mosaic flooring in place, covers the old basilica. Empress Eudocia is said to be buried under the threshold of

The Tomb of the Kings

the present church, which belongs to the Dominican Order.
It is also the centre of the French School of Biblical Archaeology.

More impressive is the Tomb of the Kings, overlooked by
the four turrets of St George's Cathedral, residence of the
Anglican Archbishop of Jerusalem. Entirely hewn out of the

rock, the sunken forecourt is reached by a colossal stairway nearly 10 metres broad; then an arched gateway opens to an inner court fronting the sepulchres. A covered porch, once beautifully chiselled with vines and acanthus leaves, protects the entrance. A narrow aperture, closed by a rolling stone, leads into a labyrinth of graves.

Some legends claim this to be the Tomb of the Kings of Judah, others that the wealthy Jerusalemite Kalba Saveya is buried here. Of Kalba Saveya the Talmud writes that 'no man, even if he were as hungry as a dog, rose from his table unsatisfied' (Babylonian Talmud, *Gittin* 56a).

Actually it appears to have been the burial vault of the royal family of Adiabene, an independent state within the Babylonian Empire around the 1st century AD. Its queen, Helena, and one of her two sons, Prince Izates, converted to Judaism, and on the death of her husband, Helena settled in Jerusalem, built a palace close to the Temple – you can see it in the Holyland model – and encouraged her country to assist the Jews in their struggle against the Romans.

French archaeologist F. de Saulcy excavated the tomb in 1850, and among the decorated sarcophagi, or stone coffins, he found one inscribed in Aramaic Sara Melaka (Queen Sara), possibly the name adopted by Queen Helena on her conversion. The finds from the Tomb of the Kings are in the Louvre Museum in Paris.

The American Colony Hotel is set in a quiet, well-grown garden in the Sheikh Jarrah Quarter. It reflects the hundred-year-old story of Horatio Spafford, a lawyer from Chicago whose wife and daughters set off to visit friends in Europe and were involved in a shipwreck in which all four girls were drowned. This misfortune awoke in the Spaffords a desire to live in the Holy Land, and in 1881 they came here with their two infant daughters. Their first home, by the Old City walls near Damascus Gate, is now an Infant Care Station.

Spacious stone-built dwellings from the late 19th century still house what remains of the American Colony people, including the Spafford grandchildren. Among other projects, they run the hotel itself, which has an unusual, attractive atmosphere, and an evening spent in its lofty, vaulted dining-room is an event you will long remember.

erusalem's Cultural Centre

s cultural centre, directly south of Binyanei Ha'uma,
ng either side of Ruppin Road – not long ago a
rossing the hills and now a four-lane highway di-
beds of colourful polyanthus roses. Here is the
campus of the Hebrew University – a townlet in
gned to replace the University on Mount Scopus
as cut off by Jordan in 1948, Givat Ram has out-
s predecessor. Together with the Mount Scopus
ince June 1967 also bustling with activity – it trains

l and University Library at the Hebrew University

Mount Scopus

Mount Scopus

The Tomb of Simon the Just, in Wadi Joz on the road to
Mount Scopus, has for generations been a place of Jewish
pilgrimage, particularly among the Sephardi communities.
Tradition holds that Simon, a member of the Great Sanhedrin in the 4th century BC, was among the City Elders delegated
to welcome Alexander the Great when he came to Jerusalem
and camped on Mount Scopus in 330 BC. From Simon's tomb,
the road ascends to the Hebrew University, passing the orderly
British War Cemetery, where Britishers who died in World
War One or while on duty in Palestine are buried.

Commanding Mount Scopus is today better known for its
association with the Hebrew University than for its strategic

position, although its military importance was acknowledged not only by Alexander and the Greeks, but by the Romans (who had a camp there), the Crusaders, the Turks and the British. Even as recently as the Six Day War of June 1967, the fact that it was already in Israeli hands favourably affected the course of victory.

When the idea of establishing a Hebrew University in Jerusalem began to take shape, the first practical step was the laying of the cornerstone on Mount Scopus immediately after World War One. Nineteen twenty-five saw the first students on the campus, and their number and choice of courses increased from year to year. Hadassah built its hospital and nursing school there in 1939, and until 1948 the place was bustling and progressive.

April 1948 saw the murderous attack on the convoy as it passed Sheikh Jarrah on the way to Mount Scopus, when seventy-eight medical and other personnel were killed. The buildings were evacuated, and although Mount Scopus itself was officially in Israeli territory, the road to it was in Jordan, so a peculiar situation arose. Under United Nations auspices, a fortnightly convoy would reach the campus, bringing food and supplies and exchanging guards. This procedure lasted until June 1967, when the approaches to Mount Scopus were taken by the Israel Defence Forces.

Today the campus is being completely rebuilt. Classes are held, and many buildings are in use, among them student hostels, the Law and Science Faculties and the imposing Truman Research Institute. Modern and functional, it includes a library and reading room, an auditorium, and rooms for meeting and study.

Apparently this area was a necropolis in Second Temple times, for in the University's Botanical Gardens a tomb with ossuaries (bone containers) was found. One bore the statement, in Greek, that 'These are the bones of Nicanor of Alexandria, who made the doors,' then two names written in Hebrew, Nicanor and Alcasa.

This may well illustrate the tale told in the Mishna (Yoma 3:10) of how Nicanor, a rich Alexandrian Jew, donated gates to the Temple. While they were being shipped a storm blew up, and to lighten the

load the captain threw one of these br he wanted to throw the second after i I will follow it!' Immediately the gale Jaffa, the first gate was found washed some twenty-five years ago, two Zioni and Menachem Ussishkin, were burie finds included an ornate sarcophagus pattern, which is now in the University' and an ossuary inscribed in Aramaic Another remarkable discovery on nearb of a crucified man, his heels still nailed

On the eastern slope of Mount to the Judean Desert and the deep Sea, is the University's magnificent auditorium, set into a curve in the the Augusta Victoria Hospital, with tower. Erected in 1910 and named German Kaiser, Augusta Victoria the British as the residence of the remained so until damaged by an it is owned by the Lutherans, who sanatorium.

The amphitheatre on Mount Scopus

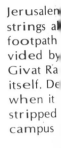

Jerusalem
strings a
footpath
vided by
Givat Ra
itself. De
when it
stripped
campus

The Natic

some 17,000 students, 4,000 of whom come from abroad, and has a teaching staff of over 2,000.

A ring road provides easy access to all sections of the campus, linking most of the buildings and projected buildings and leaving an internal traffic-free space with footpaths, covered walks, lawns and flowers. An attractive aspect of Givat Ram is the way in which use is made of decorative walls in mosaics, pottery and ceramics. Sculptures inside and out add to the University's atmosphere, the most striking being the large bronze Henry Moore mother-figure reclining near the ornamental pool and fountain. Among the buildings deserving special mention are the Administration Block, with a 7th-century mosaic pavement in the vestibule; the renowned National and

overleaf *The Givat Ram Campus of the Hebrew University*

The Billy Rose Sculpture Garden at the Israel Museum

University Library; the squat, windowless synagogue near the students'
hostels and Belgian House. This successful innovation combines a
Faculty Club and dining-hall where members can receive their
guests and includes excellent accommodation for official visitors.

One of the many remarkable achievements of the State
is the establishment of the Israel Museum. After the War of
Independence, despite the urgent problems of defence,
immigration and development, attention was soon given
to the construction of a comprehensive national museum.

overleaf *The Israel Museum above the Monastery of the Cross*

Dramatic finds and acquisitions accentuated the need for such a centre, which today stands in the midst of olive groves, where you can see a working press for olive oil like those used 2,000 years back.

The Israel Museum, architecturally one of the most functional and original of Jerusalem's new buildings, consists of four main sections: the Sculpture Garden, the Museum of Judaica and Art, the Archaeological Museum and the Shrine of the Book. Apart from a few gifts of internationally acceptable level, the Art division leaves much to

be desired. One interesting exhibit, however, is an 18th-century drawing-room, complete with curtains, tapestries and painted ceiling. Originally the salon of the Hotel Samuel Bernard in Paris, it was purchased by Baron Edmond de Rothschild, who incorporated it into his mansion in 1875. A few years ago it was donated to the Museum by the present Baron, his grandson, who also set up a $100,000 trust fund for its maintenance.

Judaica fares much better: Sabbath candlesticks; goblets, including an exquisite rhyton (or drinking horn) from the 5th century BC; spice boxes for the simple ceremony closing the Sabbath day (*havdalah*); ram's horns (*shofarim*) to usher in the Holy Days; eight-branched candelabra for the Feast of Lights (*Hanukkah*) and dozens of other items of ritual significance.

A painted booth from Central Europe recalls the Feast of Tabernacles, when the Children of Israel took 'branches of palm trees and willows of the brook . . . and dwelt in booths seven days', while the 17th-century synagogue brought from Vittorio Veneto in Italy, when its Jewish community dissolved, is a gem of its kind.

The Government Department of Antiquities, the Archaeology Department of the Hebrew University and the Israel Museum authorities (which have under their jurisdiction also the Rockefeller Museum, see page 98) have cooperated to make the Bronfman Biblical and Archaeological Museum one of the best of its kind. Arranged chronologically, it traces the story of human development in Israel through the million-year-old finds in Ubeidiya near the Sea of Galilee; through the Wadi Amun Man and the Stone Age dwellers in the Carmel caves to Canaanite days and after.

Specific to Israel and to Jewish history are the exhibits in the Shrine of the Book, sponsored by the Gottesman Foundation. Here, in cave-simulated subterranean chambers, are preserved Dead Sea scrolls and documents emanating the very essence of Judaism. Here is a copy of the Scroll of Isaiah the Prophet, writings of the mysterious Qumran hermits, and letters from the Jewish rebel Shimon Bar-Kokhba himself, a voice from the dramatic past miraculously echoing down from the year AD 130.

High buttressed walls surround the ancient Monastery of the Cross. Not long ago it stood isolated in the lonely valley where, tradition holds, the tree grew from which Jesus' cross

An exhibit at the Israel Museum

The unique architecture of the Israel Museum

was made; but today a double-level highway passes by, and two towering apartment houses dwarf its domed roof.

Now belonging to the Greek Orthodox Patriarchate, the lands were originally granted to the King of Georgia by Emperor Constantine himself. In the 11th century, the Georgians erected the present church over the ruins of an earlier one, of which part of the mosaic pavement can still be seen. Frescoes adorn the walls and column, and one of the murals shows a painting of bearded Shota Rustiveli, the 12th-century monk and Georgian national poet whose epic tale, *The Man in the Panther's Skin,* was recently translated into Hebrew by a Georgian Jew, Boris Gaponov.

How Shota Rustiveli reached Jerusalem is a story in itself. Said to have been the lover of Queen Tamar of Georgia, Shota was banished from the Georgian court when the scandal broke. He fled from his homeland, became a monk and joined the Monastery of the Cross, where he spent the remainder of his life.

Interior and exterior of the Knesset

On a hill directly north of the monastery stretch block after block of government offices, while on the summit is the Knesset – the home of Israel's parliament. The Knesset was completed in 1966, having been financed by the James de Rothschild family. Its three lower storeys burrow into the hillside. The main entrance is on the highest level, from where you go through the majestic iron gates made by David Palombo (who also made the main gates of Yad Vashem) on to a broad patio and then to the reception area. When you wish to visit the Knesset, check the appropriate hours with your hotel or the Government Tourist Information Office and take along your passport or identity card.

The focus of the reception area is the famous Marc Chagall Hall, with his series of three tapestries telling the history of the Jewish people, his wall mosaics and mosaic floor motifs. Good use has been made of Israeli artists, sculptors and craftsmen to give a rich but friendly atmosphere. You can enjoy a snack or a meal in the Knesset cafeteria, and when you leave be sure to take a proper look at the large bronze *menorah* just outside the gates. Sculpted by the British-Jewish artist Benno Elkan, this unusual piece of carving, presented by the British Parliament to its Israeli counterpart, vividly depicts fateful scenes from Jewish history.

Israel's Knesset, developing from the earlier National Council (*Va'ad Leumi*) and the State Council of April 1948, had its first meeting as an official body in Jerusalem on 14 February 1949. Today, following well-established procedures, it is composed of 120 members elected by a general vote of all citizens over the age of eighteen. At its head stands Israel's Prime Minister, assisted by a Cabinet which is directly responsible to the Knesset.

The Knesset is based on proportional representation. Democratic elections take place every four years, and among the numerous political parties, strongest up to the present has been Mapai, followed by Gahal (the right-wing Herut-Liberal Bloc), and the National Religious Party. The percentage of citizens exercising their right to vote has so far been very high, reaching over 80% at all elections.

Recently completed, the President's House in the neighbouring Talbieh district has a warm, homey feel despite its

The Van Leer Foundation's building

stately dimensions. Its reception rooms are decorated by Israeli artists, and many treasures – some of them gifts from foreign diplomats and heads of state – are on display. Glass cases also show small objects of historical interest found during excavations in the Jewish Quarter of the Old City, particularly those from the time of the Hasmonean and Herodian periods.

Adjoining the official residence of the President is the dignified white stone complex of the Van Leer Foundation and the Academy of Science and Humanities, while close by is the

A tapestry by Chagall in the Knesset

spacious and original Jerusalem Theatre with a good, kosher restaurant in the foyer. New to Jerusalem, the luxurious auditorium is being frequently used for plays, concerts, lectures and other public functions, fulfilling a need for the rapidly developing capital. These three modern buildings create an architectural grouping of which any country might be proud.

The adjacent suburb of Rehavia was founded in 1921 by European immigrants, many of them professionals and skilled craftsmen. Hard-working and ambitious, they brought with them demands for higher standards of living and a broader culture, and Rehavia did indeed develop along these

The President's Residence

lines. Today it is one of the pleasantest and most prosperous sections of Jerusalem. Building is constantly in progress there, and during the construction of a new house in Alfasi Street in 1956, a family vault, which came to be known as Jason's Tomb, was unearthed. Dating from the Hasmonean era (about the 2nd century BC), it has a single pillar upholding a pyramidal roof, while a wall drawing in the forecourt included one of the earliest known representations of a seven-branched candelabrum. An inscription records that a certain Jason was buried there, and a sketch of a merchant ship being boarded seems to indicate that piracy was the occupation of Jason's esteemed and wealthy family!

Around the Walls

Immediately outside Jerusalem's ramparts are a wealth of fascinating sites. Mount Zion, for example, lies directly south of the walls, and among its outstanding buildings are the Dormition Abbey, revered as the place of Mary's death, and the Coenaculum or Cenacle – the Hall of the Last Supper – above the traditional Tomb of David. A huge Byzantine basilica covered both places in the 5th century, but this was destroyed by the Persians in AD 614. Rebuilt by the Crusaders as two separate units, it was again destroyed, and the present abbey of the Benedictine Fathers dates only from 1900.

When you visit the Dormition Abbey, note particularly the lovely mosaic pavements and the mosaic pictures above each altar, with Mary as the central figure. Go down, too, into the dimly lighted crypt, where an image of Mary lying on a bier is circled by stone altars.

The Cenacle is allegedly the 'large upper room furnished and prepared', where Jesus ate the Passover feast together with his disciples. Of Crusader construction, it was a Franciscan monastery until 1552, when the Turks made it a mosque, adding a pulpit (*minbar*) and a prayer niche (*mihrab*). Christians were barred until 1948, when the victorious Israelis allowed freedom of worship to all.

Directly below the Cenacle is a chamber used as a synagogue, where the Tomb of David – a large stone cenotaph – is held holy. Although it is very doubtful whether this is indeed David's grave, it is believed to be a hallowed place, for it was here that one of the first synagogues was erected after the fall of Jerusalem in AD 70. Excavations revealed that beneath the present floor level was a 1st-century AD hall with an apse oriented towards the Temple Mount.

Through the cloisters of the Franciscan monastery, now grimed with the smoke of thousands of memorial candles, you reach the small Museum of the Holocaust. Here is a

The Coenaculum on Mount Zion

Mount Zion under the sign of the Covenant

synagogue and a walled courtyard covered with tablets recording the Jewish communities exterminated by Hitler.

The Church of St Peter in Gallicantu – St Peter at Cockcrow – stands on the House of Caiaphas, High Priest at the time of Jesus' execution. On the grounds is the Maccabean stairway leading down Mount Zion to Gihon, or the Silwan Spring, and on the lower level of the church is a Roman prison, complete with flagellation post and a deep dungeon.

Tradition claims that here Jesus was imprisoned by Caiaphas, and here his prophecy to Peter that 'before the cock crows

The Church of St Peter in Gallicantu

twice, thou shalt deny me thrice' was fulfilled as Peter 'sat with the servants and warmed himself at the fire'. An inscribed lintel and sets of liquid and solid weights and measures excavated in the grounds by J. Germer-Durand in 1912 indicate that this was certainly the house of a high official of Second Temple times.

Gai Ben Hinnom ('Valley of the Son of Hinnom') has at its head the ancient cistern called Birket Hasultan. Much smaller in Herodian days when it was the Serpents' Pool, it was extended by the Crusaders and again in the 16th century by

Suleiman the Magnificent, who also added the lovely *sebil* or fountain.

The valley itself had a bad reputation, for here stood the Canaanite altar of Moloch – the pagan god, made of bronze, with an ox-head and outstretched arms, who demanded child sacrifice. The priests lighted a fire inside the hollow idol and the infant was laid upon the red-hot hands! So potent was this cult that even some of the early kings of Judah succumbed to it, including the 8th century BC Ahaz, who 'burnt incense in the Valley of the Son of Hinnom, and burnt his children in the fire' (II Chronicles 28:3).

Lower down this gloomy valley, its slopes filled with rock tombs, is the Greek-Orthodox Monastery of St Onuphrius, named after a long-bearded 4th-century hermit who lived here in a cave. It is also called the Monastery of Aceldama ('Field of Blood'). The New Testament tells how Judas, after betraying Jesus, threw down his tainted thirty pieces of silver in the Temple and hanged himself. 'The priests took the silver pieces and said, it is not lawful to put them in the treasure because it is the price of blood,' and with it they bought 'the potter's field to bury strangers in. Wherefore that field is called "The Field of Blood unto this day."'

Across the valley is the attractive neighbourhood of Mishkenot Sha'ananim ('Dwelling Places of the Tranquil'), built in 1860 as the first Jewish housing outside the Old City walls. Judah Touro, a New Orleans Jew, left a bequest to be used 'for the benefit of the Jews of Jerusalem' and appointed Sir Moses Montefiore as executor. Sir Moses decided that the way to a cleaner, healthier life for the Jews of the Jewish Quarter was to move outside the walls, and, in addition to the houses, he put up a synagogue, a windmill and a small factory, laying the foundations of New Jerusalem.

Mishkenot Sha'ananim and adjoining Yemin Moshe are now being rehabilitated and transformed into luxurious, high-standard homes, for sale only to artists and people in other fields of culture, including many from abroad.

The windmill in Yemin Moshe

The Tomb of Absalom in the Kidron Valley

Valley of Kidron

Gihon – the Spring of Silwan or the Virgin's Fountain – is the only source of fresh water in the area. A decisive factor in the siting of the Canaanite stronghold and the Israelite cities that followed, it was of paramount importance during the Judean monarchy. When Assyrian troops threatened King Hezekiah's capital about 700 BC, his first thought was to safeguard the water supply!

Drawing water at the Virgin's Fountain

'Hezekiah also stopped the upper watercourse of Gihon and brought it straight down to the west side of the city of David'. This remarkable feat of engineering, during which King Hezekiah cut a 530-metre-long tunnel under the city walls and into a pool (the Pool of Silwan) within the town itself, is counted among the wonders of the ancient world. One of the 'musts' for a Jerusalem tourist is to walk through the tunnel Hezekiah bored through the rock 2,700 years ago.

Miracles still happen in Jerusalem, and one of them was the finding in 1880 of a Hebrew inscription cut into the wall of

The inscription from Hezekiah's Tunnel

the conduit by Hezekiah's workmen. It was removed, and can be seen in the Istanbul Museum. It's text reads:

Now this is the story of the tunnel:
While the workmen still lifted the pick towards each other,
And while there were still three cubits to be broken through,
The workmen called out to one another
For there was an excess in the rock to the right.
And on the day of the breakthrough
The workmen struck each towards the other, pick against
   pick.
And the waters flowed from their source to the pool
For two hundred and a thousand cubits;
And one hundred cubits was the height of the rock
Above the heads of the workmen.

More than seven centuries later, the pool became hallowed as the place where Jesus healed a blind man, and the ruins there today are those of a commemorative Byzantine church.

Gihon, the Pool of Silwan and Ein Rogel – well fed by the Gihon overflow – are all in the Kidron Valley, which is lined by a series of free-standing Second Temple tombs cut from the solid rock. At night, silhouetted by floodlighting and reflected by dark shadows, they make an unforgettable picture.

The Tomb of Jehoshaphat and Absalom's Pillar appear to form a single unit, as does the family mausoleum of Hezir and the Pyramid of Zachariah. Absalom's Pillar, with its pointed concave cone-top, probably dates from the post-biblical, Second Temple period and recalls the unhappy young man who 'in his lifetime reared up for himself a pillar in the king's date; for he said, "I have no son to keep my name in remembrance." '

Mentioned in I Chronicles 24:15, the Hezir family were priests who served in the Temple. Looking at their tomb, you find a broad, pillared porch gives on to a labyrinth of graves, and over the two central columns is inscribed in Hebrew:

This is the grave and the memorial of
Eleazar, Hania, Yoezer, Yehuda, Shimon, Yohanan
The sons of Yoseph, son of Oved;
Yoseph and Eleazer sons of Haniah, Priest of the House of
    Hezir.

Photographs of Zachariah's Pyramid before 1861 show it without the square recess at its base. Cleared by John Marco Allegro of the University of Manchester, this recess and the adjoining unfinished Tomb of Zadok are part of a present-day fairy tale, beginning in 1952 with the discovery near Qumran of a mysterious scroll incised in Hebrew on thin sheets of copper. When finally opened, it was found to contain a list of sixty-one places where treasure from the Temple was hidden away at the approach of the Romans. As far as possible, all these hiding places (including the Pyramid of Zachariah and the Tomb of Zadok) were searched, but with no results. The Copper Scroll, which had been housed in the Rockefeller Museum, was one of the few items removed by the Jordanians in the Six Day War.

Sloping up behind the Kidron Valley monuments is the Arab village of Silwan, in First Temple times the necropolis of David's City. Cut into the cliff face are graves of up to three thousand years old, often now used as stores or cattle pens. Most elaborate is the 10-metre-square stone monolith called the Tomb of Pharaoh's Daughter, the Egyptian princess who was one of Solomon's wives.

The Mount of Olives

These ancient graves are dug into the side of the Mount of Olives, facing the sealed eastern gate into the Temple compound. Jewish folklore tells that through this gate – the Golden Gate – the Redeemer will finally enter the Temple court, so that believing Jews consider it a good deed (*mitzvah*) to be buried here, to be able to follow him on the Day of Redemption.

Christians, too, hold the Mount of Olives in reverence, particularly as Jesus' last days were spent there. The mountain is covered with Christian shrines, one of them the Church of the Assumption, actually a majestic staircase descending to the crypt where Mary was buried and taken up to heaven. Originally part of a huge 5th-century basilica, it was rebuilt on a smaller scale by the Crusaders, whose point-arched, decorative gateway is worth your special attention.

A shallow cave where Israelite farmers prepared olive oil thousands of years ago used to shelter Jesus and his comrades from winter rains and summer sunshine. An oil press is called in Hebrew *gat shemen*, and from this stemmed the popular name of Gethsemane.

Antonio Barluzzi, whose name crops up over and over again in the annals of Israel's church architecture, planned the Basilica of the Agony above the remains of two earlier churches, Byzantine and Crusader. It is also called the Church of all Nations for several countries joined in rebuilding this historic monument, whose colourful mosaic pediment is a Jerusalem landmark.

Another Barluzzi gem – one of his last assignments before his death – is the Franciscan chapel of Dominus Flevit, where Jesus is said to have wept as he foresaw the downfall of Jerusalem. Entirely different is the White Russian onion-turreted church of Mary Magdalene, erected by Czar Alexander III in memory of his mother. A sad little tale recalls the Grand Duchess Elizabeth of Russia, who attended the official opening in 1888. Thirty years after, she was murdered by Russian

The Church of the Assumption on the Mount of Olives

revolutionaries, and her body now lies in the church crypt.

High up on the mountain, providing a marvellous panorama, is the luxurious Intercontinental Hotel – top grade by any standards. Below it is the peculiar semi-circular Tomb of the Prophets, bringing a gleam of Jewish tradition into the abundance of Christian holy places.

A mass subterranean cemetery where the prophets Haggai, Malachi and Zachariah are said to have been interred, it seems more likely to have been a 5th–6th-century burial ground for wealthy foreigners who died while on pilgrimage to Jerusalem. This is suggested by the fact that on excavation insciptions above the loculi (or burial niches) referred to people from Palmyra, Bithynia, Lydia, Neilah and so on. Of course, this may have been a secondary use, and the sepulchre may well be much older.

Another strange shrine is a small underground grotto revered by Jews, Christians and Moslems alike, each faith linking it with the name of a holy woman. Jews say it was the Tomb of Hulda, the 7th-century BC prophetess; Christians believe that Pelagia, a 5th-century saint, lived there, while Moslems claim it to be the modest dwelling of Rabieh el-Adawiyah, a holy woman of the 8th century.

You should also see the Eleona, or the Paternostra Church, originally erected in the 4th century by Constantine's mother, Empress Helena. A cavern where Jesus taught his disciples the Lord's Prayer is now a chapel, and the Carmelite cloister there is lined with glazed tiles bearing the text of the prayer translated into forty-four languages.

A tiny edicule with finely carved Crusader capitals covering a rock with Jesus' last earthly footprint is all that is left of the Chuch of the Ascension. In Byzantine days a large church stood there, which followed the tragic pattern of having been torn down by the Persians in 614, restored and destroyed once more by mad Caliph Hakim in 1009. The Crusaders surrounded the compound with an eight-sided wall with a circle of pillars inside, and in the middle they erected the edicule you see today. Then it was open to the sky, but in 1187 the Moslems turned it into a mosque, covering the opening with a domed roof.

Far more impressive is the tall Ascension Tower of the White Russians who do not, however, encourage visitors. If you are able to get in, look out for a chapel in the grounds with a 7th-century Armenian mosaic pavement reading:

This is the tomb of Blessed Susanna
The mother of Artevan, September 18.

The Walls and Gates

Your first glimpse of Jerusalem's crenellated walls and massive gates, each with its own special character, makes an impact never to be forgotten. Standing on foundations at least twenty centuries old, the present walls, which measure some 4 kilometres around, were built between 1536 and 1539 by Sultan Suleiman the Magnificent, the Turkish ruler under whom the Ottoman Empire reached its highest peak. In addition to using the same general outline as the Romans did, Suleiman also used their system of a north to south, and west to east axis, with good straight roads terminating in a city gate. Damascus Gate to the north, Zion Gate to the south, Jaffa Gate to the west and the Lions' Gate to the east formed the terminals then, much as they do now.

The Dung Gate – the extra opening on the southern rampart – has for thousands of years been constantly employed as the outlet for the city refuse, which has through the ages been dumped into the Kidron Valley. There are two other open entries to the north: Herod's Gate (or the Flower Gate), leading directly into the Moslem Quarter; and the simple New Gate, broken through in 1889 to give ready access to the Christian shrines. Of the blocked entrances, the Golden Gate (or Gate of Compassion) on the east facing the Mount of Olives is by far the most elaborate.

The Old City's eastern wall stretches from the Stork Tower on its northern corner to the Lions' Gate, through which the Israel Defence Forces stormed and captured the town in June 1967; then it continues along the edge of the Temple Court to the Golden Gate and on to the 20-metre-high pinnacle of the Temple. Christian tradition claims that St James the Less, first bishop of Jerusalem and brother of Jesus, was executed by being thrown from this high point. His grave is shown in the Monastery of St James in the Armenian Compound.

Two bas-relief lions, coat of arms of the 13th-century Mame-

overleaf *View of David's Tower and the Old City Wall*

luke conqueror Baybars, guard either side of the gate, giving it one of several names. Others are the Gate of the Lady Mary, for her parents' home was just inside; St Stephen's Gate, because he is thought to have been stoned to death here; and Jericho Gate, for from it the road leads east to Jericho.

The Golden Gate as you see it today, with its elaborate double portal and vestibule and its closed-off courtyard, was built during Byzantine times on the earlier gates of Herod and of Solomon and is steeped in Jewish, Christian and Moslem folklore. Jewish tradition holds that through this eastern doorway the Messiah will enter the Temple courts, so pious Jews the world over prefer to be buried on the Mount of Olives, ready for the Day of Redemption. Jesus is said to have passed through the Golden Gate to the Temple after his journey from Bethany, and through it Byzantine Emperor Heraclius carried back the Holy Cross seized by the Persian invaders.

Naturally, these messianic prophecies disturbed Jerusalem's Moslem rulers, and, as a preventive measure, the Arabs first sealed the gate in the 9th century AD. Under the Crusaders, it appears to have been re-opened only for the annual procession of pilgrims on Palm Sunday (the Sunday preceding the Easter ceremonies), but was finally blocked by Sultan Suleiman, probably when he rebuilt the walls. As an extra safeguard, a Moslem cemetery borders the eastern wall of the Temple precincts, producing a barrier of ritual impurity which the Messiah would be unable to cross!

Along the southern city wall, partly coinciding with the boundary of the Temple compound, Professor Benjamin Mazar's excavations are currently being carried out. The most recent finds have been near the line of the blocked Double, Triple and Single Gates. The Single Gate, which once led into the underground Solomon's Stables, was pierced through the massive battlements by the Crusaders in order to provide ready access to the vaults where they kept their horses. The Double and Triple Gates are on the site of the Herodian Gates of Hulda, the main entry into the Temple grounds.

The ancient Dung Gate close to the Western Wall, and

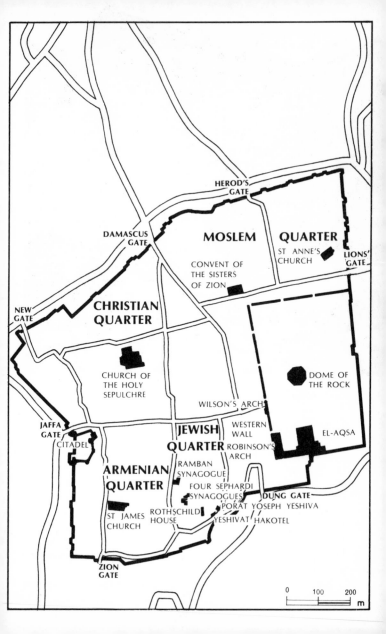

Archaeological excavations at the Southern Wall

Zion Gate, nearest the Jewish Quarter, are the Old City's southern entries. Zion Gate, close to the Tomb of David, who is also revered by the Moslems, is sometimes known as the Gate of the Prophet David. It was through this gate that the survivors of the besieged Jewish Quarter were evacuated to safety in the 1948 War of Independence.

From Jaffa Gate a road runs west to Jaffa and another south to Hebron, associated with the Patriarch Abraham, who is a holy man in Islamic as well as Jewish lore and considered by the Moslems to be the friend of God. They call Jaffa Gate Bab el Khalil ('*Gate of the Friend*'), and an inscription above it reads, 'There is no God but Allah, and Ibrahim is his friend.

Solomon's Stables

Immediately inside Jaffa Gate is one of the Government Tourist Information Offices and a large and lavish gift store. On the other side of the road is the Citadel of Jerusalem, popularly called David's Tower, embracing an amazing concentration of history in a confined space. A fortress within the fortress that is the Old City, the Citadel takes its present shape from Crusader times, although its story goes back nearly three thousand years.

Recent excavations have revealed pottery sherds and earthenware figurines from the First Temple period, and Hasmonean houses from the 2nd century BC. A city wall from that period had been found earlier, and according to the

1st-century BC historian Josephus Flavius, Herod the Great built his palace here and guarded it by three great towers 'erected into the old wall. These were for largeness, beauty and strength beyond all that were in the habitable earth.' Named for his friend Hippicus, his brother Phasael, and his lovely Hasmonean wife, Queen Mariamne, whom he murdered in a fit of jealousy, they were so outstanding that, when Roman General Titus devastated Jerusalem in AD 70, he left these towers intact 'to demonstrate to posterity what kind of city it was and how well fortified'.

Although marked on the 6th-century Madeba mosaic map, the Citadel did not play an important role during those days except as a centre of monastic life. It was the Crusaders who transformed it into a palace for the Crusader kings of Jerusalem, extending the walls and erecting many of the towers, including the large north-western tower now used as a museum.

Restored by the Mamelukes in the 14th century, the Citadel's defences were strengthened by adding the conspicuous sloping glacis to David's Tower, in reality the colossal base of Herod's Tower of Phasael, and a mosque with the familiar minaret, which has become an integral part of the Jerusalem scene. Two hundred years later the whole complex was overhauled by Sultan Suleiman and the gate-house, guard square and open-air mosque were added.

Turkish rule in Jerusalem – and in Palestine – lasted for four centuries, during which time the Citadel was the headquarters of the Turkish Army, and only in December 1917 did General Allenby proclaim the British victory from the small platform in front of the gate-house. British troops replaced the Turkish troops for the next thirty years; then from 1948 to 1967 Jordanian soldiers had their barracks there.

Since the Six Day War of June 1967 the Citadel has changed its character. Under Israeli jurisdiction it is no longer a military camp but a cultural centre, welcoming visitors from far and near with tours, exhibitions and occasional concerts. Every evening, except on the most bitter of winter nights, the Citadel's courtyard is the stage setting for the sound-and-light show called 'A Stone in David's Tower', vividly telling the fascinating story of Jerusalem.

Along the city's northern ramparts, rubble is quickly being cleared and gardens planted, embellishing ornamental Damascus Gate. Between the Christian and the Moslem Quarters, Damascus Gate stands at the head of el-Wad Street – the filled-in Tyropoeon Valley. An archaeological dig undertaken in British Mandatory times brought to light a Roman entry arch resting upon a Herodian structure.

Tradition's persistence in the Holy Land is highlighted by the name the Moslems call this gate – Bab el-Amud ('Gate of the Pillar') although there is no pillar to be seen. However, the Madeba map shows that a column did indeed stand there 1,400 years back – a fact that has never been forgotten!

The Madeba mosaic map is one of the most important sources of information on Jerusalem and the Holy Land in the 6th century AD. Probably dating from the year AD 560, the map formed the pavement of a Byzantine church in the town of Madeba in Jordan and was forgotten after the church's destruction. Discovered in 1884, when a new Greek-Orthodox basilica was built on the same site, it caused a sensation in the scholastic world, for on it were marked almost every structure or biblical site in Palestine and the adjoining countries.

Jerusalem was the focal point of the Madeba map, while the actual centre is taken as the column that once stood just inside the Damascus Gate.

Integrated into sheer rock scarp, Jerusalem's northern battlements show a half-concealed cave mouth leading into Solomon's Quarries, sometimes known as the Cave of Zedekiah, who is said to have fled from the attacking Babylonians and entered the cave, emerging from it on the way to Jericho. Actually, no outlet from the cavern has been found, but it extends beneath much of the Moslem Quarter of the Old City, and seems to have been the quarry from which Jerusalem's master builder, Herod the Great, and possibly his predecessor Solomon obtained their raw material.

Solomon's Quarries were considered one of the sights of Jerusalem in the 13th and 14th centuries. However, when Suleiman rebuilt the city walls, he seems to have sealed the entry, and it was rediscovered only in 1854 by Reverend Dr

The Rockefeller Museum

Barclay's dog, who scratched away the heaped-up earth and brought it to the attention of the public.

Opposite the eastern end of the northern rampart, near Herod's Gate, is the former Palestine Archaeological Museum, popularly referred to as the Rockefeller Museum, for John D Rockefeller Junior provided the funds for its construction and maintenance. Now it is part of the Israel Museum.

Architecturally striking, the Museum is built of smooth white stone with a central tower and open ornamental pool surrounded by a colonnade. Designed by British architect Austin Harrison and decorated with sculptures by Eric Gill, it is also functional, with fine exhibition halls, reading rooms and a library.

Some of the outstanding museum items are the models of the Hyksos (second millennium BC) graves from Jericho; Philistine human-effigy clay coffins; hieroglyphic Egyptian stelae from Beit Shean; and stucco carvings from Hisham's 8th-century palace in Jericho. Two items of special Jewish significance deserve particular attention. One is a Greek-inscribed stone fragment from the balus-

A mosaic inscription in the museum reading 'Peace upon Israel'

trade of the Court of the Gentiles in the Temple, mentioned by Josephus as having 'a partition, with an inscription, which forbade any foreigner to go in under pain of death.' This fragment, together with a complete inscription now in the Istanbul Museum, was discovered by M. Clermont-Ganneau in 1871. He found it during excavations in the Via Dolorosa near Fort Antonia, and its full text reads:

No stranger is to enter within the balustrade round the Temple and enclosure.

Whosoever is caught will be responsible to himself for his death which will ensue.

The second tablet was found on Mount Ophel – the ancient City of David – in 1914. Dating from AD 70, it is the only written evidence as yet unearthed to show the existence of a synagogue at this early date. Also in Greek, it tells that:

Theodotus son of Vettenus, priest and synagogue-president, son of a synagogue-president and grandson of a synagogue-president, has built the synagogue for the reading of the Law and the teaching of the Commandments, and the hostelry and the chambers and the cisterns of water in order to provide lodgings for those from abroad who need them.

The Armenian Quarter

Situated in the south-western section of the Old City and best reached through the Jaffa Gate, the Armenian Quarter covers one-sixth of the city's area. Its 300 acres stretch across the northern part of Mount Zion, reaching from the Citadel and David Street southward to include the high-walled, closed Armenian Compound and a broad strip of uncultivated land known as the Armenian Garden, where excavations have recently been carried out.

Within the compound is the Cathedral of St James; the Armenian Patriarchate; the Church of the Archangels and the Convent of the Olive Tree; the Church of St Theodoros, with a unique collection of original manuscripts; a secondary school; a theological seminary; a library and the earliest printing press to operate in Jerusalem.

Once the cemetery of the Armenian Patriarchs, the forecourt to the Cathedral is decorated with *khatchkars* or crossstones – plaques carved with a cross motif – brought by pilgrims in thanksgiving or in supplication. At the entrance are two strange instruments called *nakus*, relics of the days before 1840 when the ringing of church bells was forbidden and the *nakus* were struck as a summons to prayer.

Richly ornamented with wood carvings, paintings, lamps and drapings, the Cathedral of St James is dedicated to James the Less, Jesus' brother and first bishop of Jerusalem. Martyred in AD 60 by being thrown from the Pinnacle of the Temple, on the south-eastern corner of the Old City wall, into the Kidron Valley, his body, according to Christian folklore, was found in the 4th century and buried in his own home on Mount Zion. His grave is pointed out beneath the Cathedral's main altar. Another legend holds that the brother of John, St James the Major, who was beheaded by Herod Agrippe in AD 44, was also buried here under the north wall of the church. The place is marked by a small chapel.

As it stands at present, the Cathedral was probably built in the 11th century by the Georgians, then rich and powerful, who also erected the Monastery of the Cross. Major changes and additions were made in the 17th and 18th centuries and included the transfer of the main entry from the south side of the church to the west and closing off of the southern arcade, which became the Chapel of Etchmiasin.

Around the large paved patio revolves the life of the compound. Here are the living quarters of the families; the shops

The Cathedral of St James

and bakery supplying their requirements; the school and seminary; the St James' Printing Press and the Gulbenkian Library, with some 50,000 volumes of which 20,000 are in Armenian. One of the most literate and well-read people, as well as fine craftsmen, the Armenians print about 150 periodicals in their own language, in addition to countless books.

In a tranquil corner of the courtyard, the tiny Church of the Archangels stands on Byzantine remains. Thought to have been the house of Annas, high priest and father-in-law of Caiaphas, under whose authority Jesus was condemned, it is also called Deir el-Zeitunah ('House of the Olive') from the nearby tree to which Jesus was bound while awaiting trial.

Jerusalem's 3,500 Armenians, the majority of whom live within the compound, form a small but influential group. Armenian history is said to have begun when the biblical Ark came to rest on Mount Ararat, where the present lands of Iran, Turkey and Armenia meet. Hayk, from whom they are descended, came from the family of Japhet, one of Noah's three sons, while factual chronicles refer to the Armenians as far back as 600 BC.

Tigranes I, king of Armenia from 95 to 55 BC, carried out a policy of expansion which was checked by Pompey, the Roman general who also took over Palestine in 63 BC. Princes of the Herodian dynasty married into the Armenian Royal House; Tigranes IV, for example, who died in AD 35, was the grandson of Herod the Great and Mariamne, his Hasmonean wife. Tigranes V was also of Herodian-Hasmonean descent, and so was Aristobolus, who in AD 66 was the person chosen by Rome to rule over Lesser Armenia.

First to take on the Christian religion – it was accepted by the state in AD 301, twenty-five years before Rome's official recognition – Armenia also developed its own alphabet and language in 404. Today there are roughly 5 million Armenian Christians: 2.5 million in Armenia proper, one of the Soviet Socialist Republics; a million in other parts of Russia; and another 1.5 million scattered over the rest of the world, largely in the Middle East and in the United States. None, however, have as great an impact on world affairs as the handful living in the Old City of Jerusalem, to whom their fellows in the Armenian Diaspora look for leadership.

View of the Christian Quarter ·

The Christian Quarter

This quarter takes up the north-western corner of the Old City and is easily accessible either from the Jaffa Gate or the New Gate. The city walls form two of its borders, while David Street, with its host of Aladdin's Cave shops and its fruit markets, once part of the Crusader Hospital of St John, separates it from the Armenian Quarter to the south. Suq Khan ez-Zeit ('Market of the Olive Press Inn') edges it on the east. Where David Street meets the Street of the Chain, look out for the Roman Tetrapylon, now in a small café, which is a square of four pillars marking the junction of the two main Roman roads – the north–south one running through the Damascus Gate to Zion Gate, and the west–east one from Jaffa Gate to the Lions' Gate.

This is a good place to start out on a treasure hunt through the vaulted markets – an inheritance from Crusader days – where you can find quantities of blue, green and yellow Hebron glass; engraved metal plates, bowls, jugs and kettles from Iran and Arabia; ebony and mother-of-pearl inlaid boxes and furniture from Damascus; inexpensive hand-woven wool rugs and fine Persian carpets from Shiraz and Isfahan. You can find candles in all imaginable colours, delicately embroidered dresses, leather goods, candlesticks of every shape and size, crude jewellery and some of the most beautiful golden rings, bracelets and necklaces set with precious stones.

You can buy your everyday supplies there, too: groceries of all kinds, nuts, vegetables and fruit, *laban* (balls of hard white cheese in olive oil); sweet cakes with sesame seed and honey, baskets and simple furniture in Suq el-Hussar ('the Straw Market'), as well as clothing and rich, gilt-threaded material for drapings and church vestments.

At the end of David Street, three parallel roofed alleys, sometimes called Suq el-Bizar, run off to the left. They are Suq el-Lahamin ('the Meat Market'), Suq el-Attarin ('the Spice Market') and Suq el-Khawaja ('the Market of the Masters'), where wearing apparel suitable for gentlemen was once sold! Suq el-Attarin's ruler-straight continuation is Suq Khan ez-Zeit, which extends to the Damascus Gate.

'Why,' you will probably ask, 'has this section of the Old City become the Christian Quarter?' By all accounts, its story began when Emperor Constantine of Byzantium and his mother, Queen Helena, set their architectural seal upon the Holy Sepulchre in the 4th century AD. Christian institutions grew up around it, and today every sect and creed of Christianity may be encountered there. In addition to the Church of the Holy Sepulchre, also called the Church of the Resurrection, there are at least thirty churches of various denominations, and almost as many monasteries and convents, as well as schools and hostels.

Some 11,000 Christians, mostly Arabs, live in Jerusalem, and most of the sects have their headquarters in this vicinity. The Greek Catholics, the Greek Orthodox, the Latins and the Copts all have their Patriarchates in the Christian Quarter. The Greek-Orthodox Patriarchate in particular is a self-contained compound and includes three churches, the Convent of St Helena and St Constantine, a printing press, a theological seminary, a library and other facilities.

Among the Latin orders, strongest in numbers and influence are the Franciscans, whose centre is St Saviour's Convent. In addition to the monastery itself, it comprises a fine church, a pilgrim hostel, a seminary, workshops and quarters for the monks, an extensive library and a printing press of high standard. The Franciscan book store is well stocked with maps, pamphlets and religious and archaeological material, some of which is printed in their own press and unobtainable elsewhere.

Other Christian denominations to be found in the district include various Protestant sects, White and Red Russian congregations, Maronites, Ethiopians and Syrian Orthodox, whose Convent of St Mark, tucked away in a narrow lane on the outskirts of the Christian Quarter, is said to stand on the site of the house of Mary, mother of St Mark the Evangelist.

It would be impossible to describe in detail all the rituals and customs of the multiplicity of Christian creeds, but the celebration of Holy Week – the week preceding Easter – is of universal interest. The Latin Church begins its rites on Palm Sunday, the Sunday before Easter, with a service in the Church of the Resurrection and a procession from the Monastery of Bethphage, on the way to Bethany. On the following Wednesday, special day-long prayers include an early morning visit to Gethsemane.

The Maunday Thursday sacraments continue from daybreak until late evening, and among them is the mysterious ceremony of the Washing of the Feet; while Good Friday, anniversary of Jesus' crucifixion, is filled from 7 a.m. to 10 at night, and includes a pilgrimage along the Via Dolorosa and a symbolic burial service. Holy Saturday is even fuller, starting at 6.30 a.m. and ending only

The Old City market

after midnight; while Easter Sunday – the day of the resurrection –
is marked by morning worship in the basilica of the Church of the
Holy Sepulchre.

Easter for the Greek-Orthodox, the Armenian, the Coptic and the
Syrian-Orthodox churches falls a week later than the Easter of the
Latins – which is just as well, as it avoids any potential conflict over
the use of the Church of the Holy Sepulchre. Each of these sects
carries out its own special observances for Palm Sunday, Maunday
Thursday, Good Friday and Easter Sunday, but they join together
on Holy Saturday for the combined Ceremony of the Holy Fire.

Hezekiah's Pool, also called Agmygdalon ('Pool of Towers',
for its proximity to Herod's three famous towers guarding his
palace) once supplied most of the water for the irrigation of

Hezekiah's Pool

the palace gardens. You can see the Pool from the back windows of the attractive shoe stores on Christian Quarter Road. It was filled partly by rainwater and partly by the overflow water from the Pool of Mamilla, which reached it through a subterranean conduit running beneath the ramparts – a conduit that remained open until 1948.

The open space bounded by Christian Quarter Street, the Church of the Holy Sepulchre, David Street and Suq Khan ez-Zeit is called the Muristan. Two thousand years ago the Forum of the Roman town of Aelia Capitolina, it bore on it the pagan temple to Venus, destroyed by Constantine when he erected the Church of the Holy Sepulchre. Queen Eudocia, the 5th-century Byzantine empress who did so much for the Holy City, built a hospital here for the people of Jerusalem, but it was razed by the Moslems three hundred years later. The Christians built in its stead a large pilgrim hostel attached to a monastery, and a church, St Mary of the Latins. Its entrance arch is now incorporated in the Lutheran church on the spot, which has a high tower affording one of the most remarkable views in the country. The name Muristan derives from the Persian word for hospital and stems from the fact that the Crusader Knights of St John took over the monastery and turned it into a hospital again, while after Saladin's conquest in 1187, it became a mental home.

The incongruous paved road leading nowhere was part of a Turkish plan to modernize Jerusalem, and this first step was taken for Kaiser Wilhelm II's visit here in 1898. Luckily, it was never completed. Another odd sidelight on the Muristan is that some three centuries ago it became the centre for Jerusalem's tanners, and until today this is the place to buy original leather goods like handbags, travelling cases and pouffes.

The Muristan in the Christian Quarter

The Via Dolorosa

For the great majority of Christians, the high point of their pilgrimage will be the Via Dolorosa ('the Way of Sorrow'), the traditional route taken by Jesus from the Judgement Court to the place of his execution and burial. Varying from time to time through the centuries, the present Via Dolorosa, with its Fourteen Stations of the Cross, was established during the Turkish régime. Perhaps the best method of making this emotional journey is on a Firday afternoon, when at 3 p.m. the Franciscan Fathers lead a procession to the Church of the Holy Sepulchre and hold afternoon services there.

Beginning at the Lions' Gate, the only one open along the eastern battlements, look out first for the enormous Birkat Israel ('Pool of Israel') built up against the wall of the Temple

St Stephen's Gate

On the Via Dolorosa

compound. Now filled in, it was during Herodian days one of the largest reservoirs in the city.

Opposite, under the care of the White Fathers, is the Crusader Church of St Anne on the traditional site of Mary's birth-place, the home of her parents, Anne and Joachim. Simple, solid and graceful, St Anne's Church was erected by Queen Melissande, wife of Crusader King Baldwin I of

Jerusalem. A carved lintel from a 6th-century church on the same spot has been placed above the eastern doorway, while a plaque over the main entrance tells how Saladin turned St Anne's into a Moslem seminary.

Excavations in the grounds have revealed the double, colonnaded Pool of Bethesda, where Jesus is said to have healed a crippled man. The Byzantine Church of the Paralytic was built there to recall the miracle, and the Crusaders erected a chapel on its ruins.

Across the road from St Anne's, in the courtyard of the Omariyeh School, is the First Station, the Praetorium, or Roman governor's palace, where Pontius Pilate sentenced Jesus to death. Formerly this was the site of Herod's Fortress of Antonia, from where his troops protected the Temple; before that it was the Baris of the Hasmoneans, and earlier still, Nehemiah's Tower of Hananeel.

In the Convent of the Sisters of Zion you will be shown the Lithostrotus, part of the flagged courtyard of the Antonia, where crudely scratched games played by the Roman soldiers scar the paving stones. The gentle Sisters, who run a school and have organized Hebrew and Arabic study courses for adults, will give you a short explanation of the happenings here, illustrated by a model of the area. They will also point out to you the double covered cisterns of the Herodian fortress, still full of water and still in use.

Spanning the road outside the convent is the Ecce Homo Arch, mistakenly thought to be the vantage point from where Pilate proclaimed 'Behold the man!' Actually it was the eastern gate of Hadrian's town of Aelia Capitolina, built on the 'Triumphal Arch' pattern of a central and two side arches, one of which has been cleverly integrated into the Chapel of the Sisters of Zion.

A tablet set in the wall denotes Station Two, where Jesus took up the cross. Here you can visit the Franciscan Convent of the Flagellation, which has a chapel beautifully restored by Antonio Barluzzi and a small museum of finds from Dominus Flevit – the charming tear-drop church on the Mount of Olives.

Dungeons, pits and damp underground cells mark the Greek Prison of Christ, while at Station Three, a bas-relief sculpture recalls his first fall under the weight of the cross. At Station Four a Byzantine mosaic floor with a pair of sandal prints commemorates Jesus meeting with his mother. Now the Armenian Church of Our Lady of the Spasm, it is believed to stand upon the Byzantine Basilica of St Sophia.

Station Five, where Simon of Cyrene picked up the cross, is on the corner of a stepped, vaulted street in which a column set into the wall tells the story of the Lady Veronica, who, at Station Six, wiped the sweat from Jesus' brow with a kerchief. A true image of his face was left on the cloth, making it one of the most treasured and sought-after relics in the Christian world.

At the next corner (Suq Khan ez-Zeit) the place of Jesus' second fall is recorded at Station Seven, and here a segment of a red marble pillar is said to have been part of a gate of Herodian Jerusalem through which Jesus left the town. Station Eight, where Jesus told the women of Jerusalem, 'Weep

Detail of the Fourth Station of the Cross

not for me, but weep for yourselves and for your children,' is close to the Greek Convent of Charalambos, while Station Nine is marked by a column outside the Coptic Church. Ask to be shown the Cisterns of St Helena, an underground pool beneath the Coptic Church, still full of water.

Before entering the Church of the Holy Sepulchre, knock at the door of the White Russian Monastery of Alexander Miewsky and ask for permission to see the remarkable city gate and wall excavated in 1883. Dating from the Herodian era, the well-worn threshold of a large gate can be seen. This is thought to be the Judgement Gate through which prisoners were led to execution, and where the elders sat according to the injunction in Deuteronomy 16:18, 'Judges and officers shalt thou make thee in all thy gates.' The arch, of far later date, is believed to be a memorial arch, possibly once part of Constantine's Basilica of the Holy Sepulchre.

Stations Ten to Fourteen are inside the church. As it stands, it is basically Crusader, although originally built by the Emperor Constantine and his mother, Helena, in AD 335. Passing

View of the Christian Quarter

through the left-hand entry of the double doorway (the other was blocked by Saladin in 1187) you first see the Stone of Anointing of Jesus' body before burial, then, to the right, the rounded hillock of Golgotha ('the Place of the Skull'). Here are the next four stations, those of the division of Jesus' clothing, the nailing to the cross, the place of execution and the descent from the cross – all with altars richly ornamented with mosaics, paintings, carvings and silver lamps. At Station Thirteen, traditionally the Stabat Mater where Mary stood to receive her son's body, is a wooden bust of Mary covered with gold and precious jewels, thanks-giving gifts from wealthy pilgrims.

Stairs descend from Golgotha to St Helena's Chapel, below which is the cavern – the crypt of the original Byzantine church – where she is thought to have found the remnants of the cross. Between the chapel and Station Fourteen – the sepulchre itself – is the Greek Choir of Catholikon; while behind the sepulchre, just off the tiny, dim Syrian Chapel, are Second Temple tombs, showing that this had indeed been a Jewish cemetery.

When Constantine constructed the first basilica in 335, he cut away the rock from around Jesus' tomb to make it free-standing, and set it in a separate round building – the Rotunda. East of it he built the elongated Martyrion, with St Helena's Grotto as its crypt, then an entrance court to the Martyrion, then a spacious forecourt with some of its huge columns standing until today. Between the Rotunda and the Martyrion was an open court with Golgotha, exposed to the sky, in one of its corners.

The earliest Church of the Holy Sepulchre stood for nearly three centuries until destroyed by the Persian invaders under King Chosroes II in 614. Rebuilt on a smaller scale, it was again destroyed in 1009, this time by Caliph Hakim. With the coming of the Crusaders, all sections of the church were covered by one single roof and, except for comparatively minor changes, it has remained so ever since.

In the Church of the Holy Sepulchre

The Moslem Quarter

Spread over the entire north-eastern section of the Old City, the Moslem Quarter extends from Damascus Gate along the north wall to the Stork's Tower, then southward to the Street of the Chain and on to Suq Khan es-Zeit. A warren of narrow, dark lanes, relieved only by some rare specimens of 14th-century Mameluke architecture in the form of religious seminaries (*madrassas*), schools, libraries, pilgrim hostels and tombs, it is one of the most overcrowded sections of Jerusalem, old or new. Over 13,000 people, more than half the total population of the walled city, live here, many of them having come after the 1948 war and made their home in makeshift premises.

One of the most decorative of the Mameluke monuments

Detail of a gate of Suq el-Qattaim in the Moslem Quarter

is Khan el-Sultan, just off the Street of the Chain. A 14th-century hostelry, it has a two-storied passage-entry leading into a courtyard, where an Arabic inscription telling the detailed history of the khan has been set into the wall. Now dirty and neglected, the architecture shows how lovely it must once have been.

Another khan, which also served as the Market of the Cotton Merchants (Suq el-Qattaim) leads off el-Wad Street. Built in the late 14th century, its elaborate main gate opens on to the Temple enclosure and shows the typical embellishment of that period – the white, pink and black stone tracery; the recessed niches with stalactite ornamentation; the conch shell patterns and the double benches at the entry.

A curious feature of the Moslem Quarter is the fact that groups of Africans can be found throughout, generally living in the courtyards and halls of the beautiful Mameluke structures no longer fulfilling their original purpose. How did they reach Jerusalem? Apparently they were brought in by the Turks during the 16th century to replace their own bodyguards, who might have become rivals for power.

Socially rejected by the local population, the group kept very much to itself for these four centuries. Most of the Africans live in Ala e-din Street near Bab en-Nadhir, one of the western openings on to the Temple Mount, while others have made their homes in Aqabat el-Takieh, opposite the tomb of the noble Lady Tunshuq.

Other remarkable monuments of this era are the *madrassas* of Tankiziya and of Tashtamuriya and the mausoleums of the wealthy Moslem family el-Kilaniya and of Princess Turkan Khatun, who died while on a pilgrimage to Jerusalem. Both these tombs are on the Street of the Chain.

Of particularly Jewish interest is the Torat Haim Synagogue on the upper floor of a house in el-Wad Street. Founded at the end of the last century, at a time when Jews were buying property in this road as the most direct route between the Mea She'arim district and the Western Wall, it was not used since the riots of 1929. However, its Arab caretaker looked after it all through the years, and in 1967, at the conclusion of the Six Day War, he handed the keys back to the owner,

Gentlemen relaxing in the Moslem Quarter

who found everything, including a three thousand volume library, in perfect order.

Another place recently in the news is the Small Wall, which is an extension of the Western Wall and part of the Temple compound's original Herodian construction. Most is now covered by modern buildings, but at the end of Bab el-Hadid Street, adjoining Bab el-Hadid ('Iron Gate'), another of the western gates to the Temple enclosure, is an open courtyard revealing gigantic bordered ashlars of two thousand years ago.

The Dome of the Rock viewed from the Temple Mount

The Temple Mount

Often known as Haram el-Sharif, or the Enclosure of the
Noble Sanctuary, Mount Moriah, more familiarly called
the Temple Mount, is geographically within the confines
of the Moslem Quarter but spiritually it is part of the Jewish
heritage. Traditionally the site of Abraham's binding of Isaac
and of the First and Second Temples, Mount Moriah's summit
has for four thousand years been the lodestar to which all

Jews have turned in identification as they stand in worship.

At present, the sanctuary area covers 140 dunams and is completely encircled by a wall. No open gates pierce its eastern or southern wall, which are – except for one section of the southern wall – also the borders of the Old City. All entrances are to the north and west, the usual entrance being through one of the western openings, either Bab el-Mograbi ('Gate of the Moroccans'), Bab el-Hadid, or Bab es-Silselah, which is located above Wilson's Arch at the side of the Western Wall. First described by Englishman Sir Charles Wilson, this is one of a series of arches carrying an Herodian viaduct across the Tyropoeon Valley and linking the Upper City on Mount Zion with the Temple compound. Aqueducts, bringing water from the Pools of Solomon near Bethlehem to fill the capacious cisterns, were led in over this bridge, while below it halls and masonry tanks are now being cleared. One of these pool-tanks, Birkat el-Burak, is associated with Mohammed and his horse, el-Burak.

Having entered the sanctuary, you first see the Dome of the Rock, often called the Mosque of Omar, set on a broad, odd-shaped platform reached by colonnaded steps. To the right is the silver-domed el-Aqsa Mosque, and attached to it is the Islamic Museum, housing finds and records relating to Moslem history and culture. Between the two mosques is the round fountain called el-Kas ('The Cup'), where Moslems wash their hands and feet before praying.

Your first visit should be to the 43-metre-high, 50-metre-wide, octagonal Dome of the Rock, resplendent with its gleaming gold cupola and façade of cut marble and brightly coloured glazed tiles. Before entering, you will be asked to remove your shoes, and women to cover their heads and shoulders. Bring an extra pair of socks and your own scarves (those available are not to be recommended).

The Dome of the Rock is considered by some to be one of the wonders of the world. Its mosque, with a double ring of concentric columns, is indeed lovely. The mosque is filled with a rose, blue and amber glow from the stained glass windows overhead, and the inlaid ceilings, wall mosaics and thick-piled carpets combine to lend an air of tranquillity and devotion. Note that the ornamentation shows no human or animal likeness, for Islam forbids it; only decorative Arabic script and geometrical or floral patterns are employed.

Directly under the dome, surrounded by a wooden balustrade, is the round hole in the rock remarked upon by the Pilgrim of Bordeaux – the time-honoured altar of Isaac's binding and of the threshing floor of Araunah the Jebusite. Beneath is the Cave of the Souls, with four *mihrabs* dedicated to Abraham, David, Solomon and Elijah, honoured in Moslem as in Jewish lore. Below the cave, deep in the rock, is an underground cistern.

A Moslem legend tells that an indentation on the uppermost rock surface marks Mohammed's footprint. Above it, a casket holding hairs from the prophet's beard is opened annually on the 27th day of the Fast of Ramadan.

An edicule just outside the eastern door of the mosque is called the Dome of the Chain. Supported by a double ring

The Dome of the Chain. overleaf *Detail from the Dome of the Rock*

of pillars, the dome is said to have been built in the 8th century and to have acted as a treasury, on the principle that it was constantly in the public eye.

Twelve centuries of continual worship have given the Dome of the Rock a special aura. Nothing remains of the simple wooden structure put up by Caliph Omar in AD 638, but the present mosque is basically the same as that erected around 690 by Caliph Abd el-Malik. Its architectural history is one of repair and restoration, the first being carried out in

Interior of the El-Aqsa Mosque

830 by Caliph el-Mamun, who removed the name of Abd el-Malik from the mosaic inscription and put his own instead!

Both Saladin in 1187 and Suleiman the Magnificent after the Turkish conquest rebuilt it, while most recently, in the five years between 1958 and 1963, the Jordanian Government carried out structural changes; renewed the tiling and wood-work, and replaced the 200-ton lead dome by a comparatively light-weight bronze-and-aluminium alloy one made in Italy and weighing only 35 tons. An unvouched-for rumour in-sists that the new dome was lowered into place by helicopter.

El-Aqsa's broad, low façade of seven arches gives on to a covered portico. On the left of the porch, a stairway leads down to ancient Aqsa, where deep vaulted passageways from the time of the Second Temple are said to connect with the Double Gate, one of the ancient Hulda Gates now being excavated.

The inside of the prayer hall gives a deceptive impression of modernity, for the marble columns have recently been restored, the flooring replaced and the wooden beams freshly painted. The mosque was, in fact, originally built around AD 710 by Caliph Ibn Abd el-Malik, the son of the ruler who erected the Dome of the Rock, on foundations believed to have once supported Solomon's Palace and the Palace of the Kings of Judah.

Numerous legends have grown up around this strange and often-rebuilt spot. One of them tells how the murderers of 12th-century Thomas à Becket, Archbishop of Canterbury, came to Jerusalem to do penance for their sins, died in exile and were buried just inside the entrance to the el-Aqsa mosque, in the so-called Tomb of the Sons of Aaron. A new folktale came into being in 1969, when a crazed tourist attempted to set fire to the mosque. Some damage was done, including the destruction of an exquisite ebony and ivory pulpit made in Damascus in 1168 and installed here in 1187, but apart from that the effects were negligible.

One of the most fascinating corners of Mount Moriah is that on the south-east, where tremendous flagstones cover part of its water storage supply and where the supporting vaults of Herod's extension of the foundation platform form the mysterious subterranean labyrinth of Solomon's Stables. The Crusaders utilized this vast space for stabling their horses, breaking through the now-blocked Single Gate to provide easy access.

Before you leave, take a last look around the Enclosure of the Noble Sanctuary and recall the fateful changes that have overtaken this tiny spot during its long and eventful history from the time David 'built there an altar unto the Lord', and Solomon erected his lovely Temple above it. This was replaced by the magnificent Second Temple of Herod, who expanded the building area by the skilful employment of strong supporting arches, now the subterranean Solomon's Stables. Remains of Herod's work can still be seen in the Western Wall – a symbol of unity for Jews the world over.

Rome's destruction of the Temple on the 9th of Av in AD 70, strengthened the bonds between the Jew and his homeland. Banished from Jerusalem, Jews were permitted to return only on the anniversary of that dreadful day when, as the Pilgrim of Bordeaux recorded in AD 333, they clustered round 'a perforated stone, which they anoint, bewail themselves, rend their garments and depart'.

An abortive effort to restore the Temple was made in AD 361 by the apostate Roman emperor Julian, who hoped it would help him in his struggle against the rising tide of Christianity. Some catastrophe struck the materials prepared, and a superstitious fear prevented another attempt being made. The site remained untouched until Caliph Omar conquered Jerusalem and erected a wooden mosque under the Temple Mount.

About fifty years later the Dome of the Rock was constructed, its gold-gleaming cupola forming a landmark on the Jerusalem scene. A second landmark was the silver-capped el-Aqsa mosque, taken over during Crusader rule as the headquarters of the Knights Templar, while the Dome of the Rock became the church known as Templum Domini ('Temple of the Lord'). Saladin in 1187 turned the Haram once more into a Moslem sanctuary, and so it has remained ever since.

The Jewish Quarter

Located in the south-eastern corner of the Old City, the Jewish Quarter is the smallest of walled Jerusalem's well-defined districts. Most of it is situated on the eastern slope of Mount Zion reaching down to the Tyropoeon Valley and the Western Wall – the site of the ancient Upper City, where the palatial homes of the Hasmonean and Herodian nobility helped to make Jerusalem of those days one of the most beautiful cities in the world.

Until recently it was generally accepted that development on this part of Mount Zion began only from the 3rd century BC under Greek influence. However, Professor Nahman Avigad's excavations there have revealed, among a host of other exciting finds, and 11-metre stretch of a city wall from the 8th–7th centuries BC – clear evidence that there was Jewish habitation here during the period of the First Temple.

Following Nebuchadnezzar's conquest in 586 BC, Jerusalem was desolate for some fifty years, when Babylon in turn was conquered by the Persians. King Cyrus encouraged his Jewish citizens to return to their homeland, and a small group under Sheshbazzar, a prince of the house of Judah, came back and restored the practice of worship in the Temple courts.

Difficulties were overwhelming, and only with the coming of Nehemiah, the Persian king's cupbearer and courtier, around 445 BC did matters improve. Nehemiah, who came to Jerusalem with the king's blessing and guarded by royal troops, found 'the walls of Jerusalem broken down and the gates thereof consumed with fire'. He was soon joined by the scribe and prophet Ezra, and together they organized the rebuilding of the capital, which grew and prospered through Greek domination and the rule of the Hasmoneans. It reached a climax of wealth and beauty during the reign of Herod the Great, when its population reached a quarter of a million and its area was roughly four times that of the present-day walled town.

Disaster followed. Rome's vicious destruction of the Temple

and of Jerusalem in AD 70 was a turning point in the fortunes of the Jewish nation; but despite the pillage and slaughter carried out by the Roman troops, a flicker of nationalism still remained. It burst into flame when, in AD 132, Shimon Bar-Kokhba rallied Jewish forces around him and retook Jerusalem.

This last glimmer of freedom was quenched in AD 135. All the might of Rome was brought up against the handful of Jewish rebels, who were driven from Jerusalem and from their cave refuges in the Judean Desert, then besieged and killed in the hill-fortress of Betar, now the Arab village of Battir.

Roman emperor Hadrian, commander of this action, decided to make an end of Jewish Jerusalem once and for all. He banished all Jews from the city, broke down and ploughed over its walls and built over its ruins the small square town of Aelia Capitolina. The total ban on Jews lasted for nearly two hundred years, then it was gradually relaxed and they were permitted to come once a year, on the 9th of Av, the anniversary of the destruction of the Temple, to mourn their glorious past and lament at the ruins of their Temple.

With Emperor Constantine's adoption of Christianity, Jerusalem took on another aspect. It regained its historic name and its importance, for it was now also the Holy City of the Christian faith and a centre of Christian, as it was of Jewish, pilgrimage. The position of the Jews eased a little more, and under the 5th-century AD empress Eudocia, who also expanded the city walls to include part of Mount Zion, they were even encouraged to settle in Jerusalem.

This was the time when the Jewish Quarter really started, for the returning Jews probably chose to be as close as possible to their ancient shrines – the Western Wall and the Temple Mount. Conditions for the Jews were improved under the Moslem occupation of AD 638, and from this juncture the story of the Jewish Quarter is that of its synagogues.

First to be built here, in the Street of the Karaites, was the traditional Karaite Synagogue of the Karaite Jews. Immigrating

A reconstructed building in the Jewish Quarter

from Babylon under the leadership of Anan ben David in AD 767, this strange sect of Jews believes only in the Pentateuch and thus celebrates neither Purim nor Hanukkah. A number of them still remain in Israel, although none are left in Jerusalem.

Their curious underground synagogue is now undergoing a complete but slow job of restoration. Reached by a flight of steep, narrow stairs descending from a small courtyard with a wealth of Hebrew memorial inscriptions, the subterranean halls are lighted by only a few chimneys in the arched roof. It has a ritual bath in the basement and a number of extra side rooms for various purposes. Although the synagogue appears to be very old, neither documentary nor archaeological findings suggest that it is any earlier than medieval.

At some period before the Crusader era, possibly during the 10th or 11th centuries, the Jewish Quarter seems to have moved from the south-eastern to the north-eastern corner of the Old City, where the Moslem Quarter stands today. Here it was that the Jewish inhabitants of Jerusalem clustered together on the fateful morning in the summer of 1099 when the Crusaders broke through the defences of the city, massacring every Jew and Moslem they encountered until the streets ran ankle-deep in blood.

Neither Jews nor Moslems were allowed to return to Jerusalem, but despite this decree a few individuals managed to filter in and, being skilled craftsmen, were allowed to stay. A Jewish pilgrim, Rabbi Benjamin of Tudela, came to Jerusalem around 1167 and found a company of two hundred Jews, all dyers, who 'dwelt in a corner of the city under the Tower of David'. Some years later, however, their number had dropped to two.

After Saladin's defeat of the Crusaders in Jerusalem in 1187, conditions were far better. Jews were permitted to settle in the town, but life was hard, and the numbers in the Jewish Quarter grew very slowly until in 1267, when a Spanish Jew, Rabbi Moses Ben Nahman (the Ramban) arrived in Jerusalem after tangling with the Spanish Government. He established the synagogue which is still in use in the Street of the Jews, and of it he wrote to his son, 'It has marble pillars and a fine cupola', giving the impression of a grand hall.

Later reports rather change the picture, for in 1488 Rabbi Ovadia of Bartenura describes the synagogue of Jerusalem – the Ramban – as being without a cupola, 'long, narrow and gloomy, with no light except from the entrance', while Rabbi Moses Basula writes in 1523 that 'there is but one synagogue in Jerusalem . . . a beautiful synagogue with four pillars in a row'. Excavations now in process show that the line of columns does

A reconstructed synagogue in the Jewish Quarter

extend, as was believed, but they are squat, with unmatched capitals, and set on a floor level a little lower than it is today. The general theory seems to be that this was probably a kind of hostel-cum-stable for the Crusaders with their horses and equipment, quickly fixed to provide them with shelter as they rode up from the coast.

Incidentally, of the sixty or so synagogues and other religious institutions flourishing in the Old City before 1948, only this one was left reasonably intact, possibly because of the mosque in its courtyard. The four Spanish synagogues grouped as a unit were not actually destroyed, but they were looted and used as cattle byres by the Jordanians, while most of the others were blown up.

Jerusalem's Jewish population of a few hundred among some 10,000 inhabitants was reinforced by Spanish refugees escaping from the Inquisition. Arriving at the very end of the 15th and the beginning of the 16th centuries, they brought with them many of the customs and the arts of cultured Spain, and one of their first collective actions was to erect the Synagogue of Elijah the Prophet, which was completed in 1516.

The Synagogue of Rabbi Yohanan Ben Zakkai was soon built adjoining the earlier one. A dignified and lofty hall, with a women's gallery reached from street level, it has a double Ark, ornamental discs to neutralize the forbidden cross of the ceiling vaulting and an imitation *mihrab* on the outside. This was added during one of its many restorations to lull the Turks into thinking it was a mosque, thus preventing any contemplated disturbance of religious services!

Later still, the spacious Istanbuli Synagogue, with its four square columns and high dome, was added; then the entrance courtyard common to all three, which also included the ritual bath for the whole complex, was roofed over and decorated to provide another prayer room.

Restoration of the complex was undertaken jointly by Jerusalem's Sephardi community, the Jerusalem Municipality and well-wishers from abroad, including the Rothschild family from London. The festive opening took place on 25 September 1972, during the Feast of Tabernacles, and was particularly moving as this was the first of the Old City's synagogues to be rehabilitated after the Six Day War.

The Hurva Synagogue. overleaf *Restored Yohanan Ben Zakkai Synagogue*

The year 1699 saw a big influx of Jews into the Jewish Quarter, for Rabbi Yehuda the Hassid came from Poland with a company of eight hundred disciples. They immediately planned for a large Ashkenazi place of worship, obtained the land near the Ramban Synagogue and began to build. But Rabbi Yehuda died, and without his initiative no progress was made. Abandoned for 150 years, the abortive project became known as Rabbi Yehuda's ruin (*Hurva*).

Even after its completion in 1864, the name Hurva clung to it, although for nearly a century it was one of the most beautiful buildings in the country. Now it is again a ruin, for all that remains after the Jordanians dynamited it in 1948 is a single high wall and part of the marble pulpit.

Also among the synagogues devastated by the Arab Legion is the rubble-filled Tiferet Israel, still showing a façade of three ornamental arches. Founded by Israel Bek of Safed, who came to Jerusalem in the middle of the last century and started the first Jewish printing press in the city, it was completed by his son, Nissan, in 1872. This lovely synagogue cries out for restoration!

Yeshivat Hakotel, Batei Machse and the Rothschild House, with the Rothschild coat of arms above the entrance, form an unusual complex. Erected during the latter part of the 19th century on what was once the headquarters of the Teutonic Knights, these attractive apartments were financed by Jewish groups from Europe and let to newcomers at low rents for a maximum of three years.

During the 1948 siege of Jerusalem, Rothschild House, with its wide courtyard, acted as a centre for the beleaguered citizens. Many met their death here and were buried in a common grave; then, only after the Six Day War, were the bodies transferred to the cemetery on the Mount of Olives.

Near the Yeshivat Hakotel, which is housed in a section of the Batei Machse, is the apse of an enormous, thick-walled Byzantine basilica thought to be the Nea of Emperor Justinian, while placed around the courtyard are architectural fragments from the archaeological dig in the immediate vicinity. Stately pillars, with broad bases and richly carved capitals, found

Rothschild House in the Jewish Quarter.

here – in the Upper City of Second Temple times – might even have been part of the lavish Hasmonean Palace, from where Herod Agrippa II and his sister, the lovely Princess Berenice, spoke to the people of Jerusalem on the eve of the Temple's destruction.

An interesting sidelight on the Jews of Jerusalem comes from the official population figures over a period of years, for when the Hurva was built, Jerusalem's 10,000 Jews comprised half its population. For the next forty years the numbers steadily increased to about 40,000, the proportion of Jews remaining the same. With the Russian pogroms of the early 1900s came a wave of immigration, and in 1905 Jews accounted for two-thirds of Jerusalem's 60,000 citizens.

After a setback due to the economic difficulties of the post-war years of 1919 to 1921, Jews quickly regained their majority in the city, and by 1948 they numbered nearly 100,000 in a

The archaeological excavations in the Jewish Quarter

count which registered 40,000 Moslems and 25,000 Christians. By 1967, after the Six Day War, the Jewish population had almost doubled, while the non-Jewish population remained practically stationery at around 70,000.

Newest of Professor Avigad's discoveries during his work in the Jewish Quarter of the Old City is a luxurious mansion of Herodian days (about the 1st century BC). Located just inside the Zion Gate, its open patio, painted frescoes and mosaic floors point to its owners having been a wealthy Jewish family.

Professor Avigad's earlier excavations are concentrated in two areas very close together. One is immediately behind the Ramban Synagogue, and many remarkable finds were made here, including painted frescoes and carvings from Herodian days. That of the seven-branched candelabrum (*menora*), thought to have been copied from the golden candlestick in the Temple, was a unique discovery.

Towers, cisterns, water conduits, pottery and coins from the Hasmonean era were also unearthed, as well as remains of structures, pottery sherds and Astarte figurines from the 7th century BC, the days of the First Temple.

The second area in Misgav Ladach Street, barely 170 metres across from Robinson's Arch, brought with it more startling results, especially that of the broad wall from the 7th century BC. The wall will be preserved and eventually exhibited beneath the structures rising on the site.

Another sensational find was the Burnt House, also soon to be open to the public. This was a house and workshops from the 1st century AD that was burnt by the Romans after the fall of the Temple on the 9th of Av in AD 70. Even the exact date of this horrible happening is known, from Josephus' writings, for the Upper City fell exactly one month after the destruction of the Temple, and it was set afire 'on the eighth day of the month Gorpieus (*Elul*)'.

Archaeological evidence shows this to have been a moderately large house, with a kitchen and a basement, ovens, various utensils, stone vessels of a type found only near the Temple Mount in Jerusalem and sets of weights and measures. On one of the weights was scratched the name Bar Katros – the surname of a priestly family attending to Temple rites.

The Babylonian Talmud (*Pesahin* 57a) relates how this particular family carried out its duty as tax collectors without mercy, often sending their servants to whip defaulters who were late in paying.

A single sign of a human presence was uncovered in the bones of a girl's forearm found grasping the highest cellar stair, as if attempting to pull herself up from the smoke and flames. After two thousand years, this tragic incident is as moving as if it had happened yesterday!

The entrance to this amazing museum *in situ* is already marked – it is in Misgav Ladach Street and will be beneath the temporary premises of the *yeshiva* and synagogue of Porat Yoseph, which stand among the arches and vaulted roof of a Crusader monastery.

The Western Wall

The Western Wall is the symbol of the Jews' unwavering faith in their beliefs and in their homeland. Spiritually it is a symbol, physically it forms part of Herod's massive ramparts supporting the Temple platform and, as the last remaining fragment of the House of God, is still a magnet for Jews the world over. Since the Temple's destruction it has been customary for Jews to gather there, especially on the 9th of Av, anniversary of the destruction, to pray at the tear-washed stones and mourn the nation's vanished glory.

Even under the harsh rule of Aelia Capitolina, when for nearly two hundred years no Jew was allowed to set foot in the city, a blind eye was usually turned during this fateful day, and Jews often managed to approach and worship at the sacred shrine. Only from 1948 to 1967, while the Jordanians were in control, were the Jews entirely cut off, making the reunion of 7 June 1967 one of the most remarkable moments in Jewish history.

Immediately after the liberation of the Old City the slum houses overlooking the Western Wall were cleared away, and a wide space for mass gatherings opened up. An unwelcome innovation introduced by the Ministry of Religious Affairs was the separation of men and women worshippers – an arrangement never previously practised.

Looking at the Western Wall today, you find it extends for some 75 metres from the Gate of the Moors on the right to Wilson's Arch on the left. Named for Sir Charles Wilson, this was actually a section of a viaduct connecting the Upper City to the Temple Mount across the Tyropoeon Valley and also formed part of the Hasmonean city wall. Over its eastern end stands Bab es-Silselah, while beneath it, spacious chambers have been cleared of dirt and rubble and turned into a synagogue.

On the right, note particularly the colossal lintel of Barclay's Gate or the Gate of the Prophets. About $2\frac{1}{2}$ metres high and at least 10 metres long, it was during Second Temple times also called the Kiponus Gate. The Mishnah (*Middot* 1:3) mentions it among the five gates to the Temple Mount.

The Western Wall itself is beautifully built of 1¼ metre high, 4 to 9 metre long, neatly bordered ashlars, each course fractionally set back from the one below to make it strong and stable without depending upon mortar or any type of binding material. Twelve layers of this fine Herodian masonry rise above ground level, and there are another eighteen below, while the two-thousand-year-old stones are topped by four metres or so of inferior Turkish building. One day in the future, when the Western Wall is cleared to its foundations, it will reach the impressive height of some 44 metres!

All these underground details were discovered in 1867 by Sir Charles Warren of the British Royal Engineers. Sponsored by the Palestine Exploration Fund, Warren sank deep shafts close to the Wall, then dug out horizontal tunnels at varying levels. One of his shafts, illuminated and protected, is under Wilson's Arch, and you can look down to bedrock and see the heavily margined, distinctive rock-cut blocks of the retaining wall's foundations.

To the right of the Gate of the Moors you can see the springing of Robinson's Arch, named for the American

Robinson's Arch

archaeologist who first described it. Here Professor Mazar started his excavations in February 1968 – excavations which aroused world-wide interest, and have progressed to be the largest-scale dig ever undertaken in Israel, spreading over some 30 dunams. A special arrangement has recently been made by which, for a nominal fee, a guide will show you over the site. Just phone the project office – (02) 84669 – for an appointment. A morning spent there will be an unforgettable experience!

Majestic tombs from the time of the kings of Judah (about the 7th century BC) were found dug into the hillside directly west of Robinson's Arch. It seems likely that when the city was extended in the 2nd and 1st centuries BC, the human relics were reburied further afield and the ground used for building.

Many finds were made, but of greatest significance are those from the Second Temple era, which included a 13 metre wide road running parallel to the Western Wall along the Tyropoeon Valley and then down to the Pool of Silwan. Beneath it was the conduit discovered originally by Warren, which led off the surplus water from the Temple enclosure's cisterns into the pool. Branching from the broad, paved road was another one bordering the southern wall of the Temple compound. Even more beautifully paved than the main street, its surface of smooth marble slabs was cracked by coping-stones tumbling from the battlements during Titus's attack in AD 70.

From the nearby south-west corner fell an 80 ton stone block with a niche in it large enough for a man to stand in, and an inscription chiselled along its margin read, in Hebrew lettering, 'Le veth Hatiqiyah' ('The Place of Trumpet Blowing'). On this parapet, it seems, the priest stood when he announced the coming of the Sabbath and of the High Holy Days by trumpet blast.

Recently a 90 metre wide stairway edging the south wall was uncovered. It led up from the ancient town on Mount

A celebration at the Western Wall

View of excavations at the Western Wall

Ophel to the twin Gates of Hulda, one of which stood on the site of the present blocked-up Double Gate and the other on the site of the Triple Gate. The Hulda Gates were those used by the mass of the people, who swarmed into the Temple compound not only to participate in prayer and sacrifice, but to meet their friends and attend talks and discussions in the Temple courts.

During the three Pilgrim Festivals of Passover, Pentecost and Tabernacles, tens of thousands streamed into the capital. Inns and hostels were full to overflowing, and areas outside the walls were often allocated as communal campsites.

The Mishnah (*Middot* 1:3) tells that 'the two Hulda Gates on the south served for coming in and for going out', and explains further (in *Middot* 2:2) that 'whosoever it was that entered the Temple Mount came in on the right

and went around and came out to the left, save any whom aught befell, for he went round to the left'. In this way the elders sitting at the gate knew that something was amiss, and the tractate goes on to give a typical conversation: 'What aileth thee that thou goest to the left?' 'Because I am a mourner.' 'May he that dwelleth in this House give thee comfort!'

Another recent discovery revealed that Robinson's Arch, long thought to have been a second viaduct linking the Upper City with the Temple, consisted of one huge single arch, 15.5 metres in width, leading off the Royal Stoa (the covered porch along the top of the south wall), then making a right-angled turn down a regal staircase to the broad piazza. The first clue that this was not a bridge came with the discovery of a series of graduated arches which proved to be the profile of the staircase. Set into it at ground level were four recessed chambers opening on to the street, which are believed to have been shops supplying the requirements of Temple visitors. The mixture of coins found nearby indicates that the money-changers did a brisk trade.

Six courses beneath the inset of Robinson's Arch, a Hebrew inscription was unearthed cut into one of the ashlars. Taken from Isaiah 66:14, it reads: 'And when you see this your heart shall rejoice, and your bones shall flourish like the green grass.' It is incised in antique-style, square Hebrew script and was probably written in AD 361 during the reign of Emperor Julian the Apostate. Julian attempted to restore the Temple – an attempt which came to a disastrous end.

Later architectonic remains are those of Byzantine structures, including luxurious two-storied houses with fine mosaic floors and the fragments of rich utensils – lamps, bowls and glass vessels – and of the great palace of the early Arabs. From these impressive relics it can be deduced that after the Moslem invasion of AD 638, the Ommayad ruling family followed the erection of the Dome of the Rock by the building of this huge mansion with bath-houses and pillared courtyards.

Several inscriptions, apart from the two already mentioned, were found in the dig. One, part of a pillar bearing the name of Vespasian, had been reused in the Ommayad palace; and another – a tablet written in Arabic – stated that the palace was built in AD 701.

The miscellaneous finds included two sun-dials which had been incorporated into the south wall, numerous coins from the Hasmonean right through to the Turkish period, statuettes in bronze and earthenware, pottery lamps, dishes, juglets and stone containers. Of special interest is a fragment of a small stone vessel incised with a sketch of two birds and the word *'Korban'* ('Sacrifice'). Professor Mazar considers it may have a direct link with the ritual purification of a woman following menstruation, when Leviticus 15:29 instructs that 'On the eighth day she shall take unto her ... two young pigeons, and bring them unto the priest'.

The Jerusalem Theatre

Entertainment and Restaurants

Before leaving Jerusalem for excursions into the administered territories, it is well to bear in mind that you should aim to be back in town by nightfall. You can start early in the day, and if you take with you a flask of tea or coffee and some biscuits in winter, or cold drinks in summer – perhaps a picnic basket, too – your enjoyment will be doubled.

On your return, a shower and change of clothes will freshen you up in preparation for a pleasant evening in Jerusalem. Hechal Shlomo, for example, extends a warm welcome to tourists coming to its Oneg Shabbat function held every Friday night, as well as to the traditional Melave Malka, which closes the Sabbath day.

Music is tremendously popular in Jerusalem, and in addition to the Israel Philharmonic concerts and special musical events, the Broadcasting and Chamber Music Orchestra perform weekly. Theatre is fast becoming part of life in Jerusalem, and the fact that the capital now possesses a handsome, comfortable playhouse, where you can also dine in luxury, has been a big step forward. Some excellent shows are put on at the theatre itself, at the small but attractive Khan (which also has an attached restaurant) and occasionally at Binyanei Ha'uma.

Tuesday is the day when the Israel Museum is open until 10 p.m., and if you were busy sightseeing during daylight hours, this is an ideal time to wander around the Museum exhibits and to have a snack in its excellent cafeteria. However, if you are looking for a livelier set-up, you can ask your hotel to book a place at the Khan's night-club, at Soramello's or at the Abu Tor discotheque.

If you would rather enjoy a good meal in pleasant surroundings, although Jerusalem lags a long way behind Tel Aviv in terms of eating out, there are today many good – and some excellent – restaurants. Most of the big hotels have regular and dairy-food restaurants (notably 'La Regence' at the King David, the Intercontinental, the Diplomat and the American Colony), and some of the other restaurants worth trying are:

West Jerusalem (kosher restaurants marked with a *)

Pe'er (French); Gondola (Italian); Goulash Inn, Ein Karem (Hungarian); Chez Simon (French); Jerusalem Theatre* (European); Fefferberg* (traditional Jewish); Gerlitz* (traditional Jewish); Palmach* (Oriental); Beni (fish); Hesse* (European); Mandarin (Chinese); Alpine* (vegetarian); Finks (European in a British pub atmosphere); Citadel (European); the Khan (European); Pundak Motza at the village of Motza just outside Jerusalem on the main Tel Aviv highway (Oriental and European).

East Jerusalem (all Oriental food unless indicated, and all non-kosher)

Arabesque; Jerusalem Oriental Restaurant; Hassan Effendi; Masswadeh; Golden Chicken; Sea Dolphin (fish); Hazvi (Oriental and sea food); Gino, inside the Christian Quarter of the Old City (Italian).

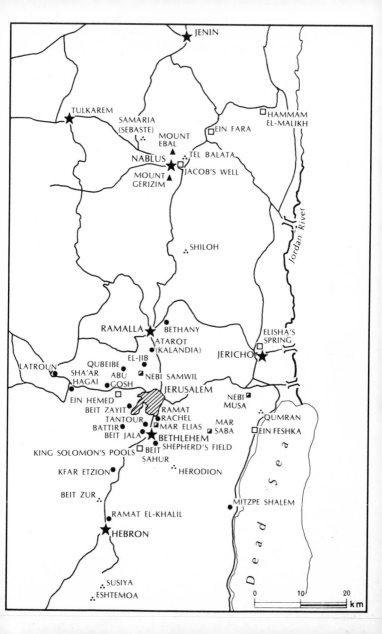

Judea and Samaria

East of the Watershed the land drops away rapidly through the Judean Desert to the Dead Sea and the Jordan Valley. Throughout the ages, this trackless wasteland has been a refuge for those fleeing from persecution, as Hagar fled from the anger of Sarai, her mistress, and King Zedėkiah from the Babylonians, who 'overtook him in the plains of Jericho'. Later it became the haunt of monks and hermits, the earliest of them being

The Judean Desert

the Essenes, who lived at Qumran on the shores of the Dead Sea from the 1st century BC to the 1st century AD . During Byzantine days, the hills were dotted with anchorites' cells and with monasteries, some of which exist to this day.

The road from Jerusalem to Jericho is a journey through history. Bethany, a favourite pilgrim centre, was the home of Lazarus and his sisters, Mary and Martha – a home where Jesus was a frequent and welcome guest. Here he would gather a group around him for discussions, and while Mary 'sat at Jesus' feet, and heard his word, Martha was cumbered about

Bethany

The road from Abu Dis to Beit Sahur

much serving'. Complaining that Mary did not help her, Martha was told in no uncertain terms what was more important.

The New Testament story goes on to tell how Lazarus died, and how, after he had been dead four days, Jesus restored him to life. His tomb is shown behind the Franciscan Sanctuary of St Lazarus – yet another Barluzzi masterpiece – which incorporates 4th-, 6th-, and 12th-century remains. Of particular interest is the ruined medieval watchtower guarding the Crusader Convent of Queen Melisande of Jerusalem, and the huge olive press attached to the modern monastery.

For the more adventurous, monasteries of the past and of the present can be found off the main highway to the right and left. On the bleak, spectacular and desolate road linking the village of Abu Dis,

just past Bethany, to Beit Sahur, you reach the rebuilt Church and Monastery of St Theodosius, where the Three Wise Men from the east rested after paying homage to the infant Jesus in Bethlehem. You can also reach the church by turning into the Beit Sahur road leading off left from the entrance to Bethlehem. Look out for the remarkable 5th-century clover-leaf apse in the church and for the crypt where skulls of dead monks are piled into one section and their bones in another. Rock-cut sarcophagi ornamented with crosses and rosettes are said to be the graves of early Christian notables, including St Theodosius himself, who died here in 529 at the great age of 105.

An unpaved track from the Church of St Theodosius takes you to the Monastery of Mar Saba, mentioned five hundred years ago in Fr. Felix Fabri's journal as 'one of the most wondrous things I have seen in all my travels'. Set on the scarp of a steep cliff in the depths of the Kidron Valley, it is enclosed by gigantic ramparts, while a great buttressed wall supports the side overlooking the canyon. In the caves around, hermits lived their solitary lives, meeting only for communal prayer, thus forming what is known as a 'Laura'. Women are not allowed to enter the grounds, and must be content to watch the menfolk of the party go through the low arch into the courtyard roofing the monks' burial vault. A small edicule marks where Mar Saba was buried in AD 533.

The domed Church of St Saba houses the mummified skeleton of Saba himself dressed in gorgeous robes. Taken from the original grave in 1256 and transferred to Venice for safety, it was returned here at the request of Pope Paul VI after his visit to the Holy Land in 1964. Adjacent is St Nicholas' cave-chapel where, behind an iron grille, you can see the skulls of hundreds of monks murdered by the Persians in AD 614.

Saba was a remarkable man. Born in 439 AD in Cappadocia, now Central Turkey, he travelled with his friend and compatriot, Theodosius, to Jerusalem and in the course of time set up this monastery. It became the centre for the anchorites (solitary-living monks) as the nearby Monastery of Theodosius was the centre for the cenobites (communal-living monks), and at the height of its activity, some five thousand anchorites would converge on St Saba's Monastery for mass worship.

Built around 485 AD, it was repeatedly destroyed and rebuilt until taken over by the Greek-Orthodox Patriarchate, and eventually, with Russian help, was rebuilt in 1840 in the form it has today. Despite these ups and downs, the Mar Saba library and manuscripts were among the finest in the world, and when transferred to the Greek-Orthodox Patriarchate in Jerusalem, priceless writings were found, including some of Cyril of Scythopolis (Beit Shean), of John of Damascus and of one of the earliest copies of the Septuagint – the 3rd-century BC Greek translation of the Old Testament.

A track bearing left – that is, northwards – from kilometre-stone 15 on the Jerusalem–Jericho highway takes you to the head of Wadi Kelt, near Jeremiah the prophet's birthplace,

Mar Saba

Anatot. Here is the White-Russian Monastery of Ein Fara, located at the abundant spring of Ein Fara, one of the three rich water sources of Wadi Kelt (the others being Ein Fawwah and Ein Kelt).

One of the monks of Ein Fara, early 5th-century St Euthymius, became the moving spirit in the establishment of hermitages right through the Judean Desert. His particular monastery, now ruined, served the double purpose of being a monastic centre and a khan for travellers – a combination frequently encountered. Interesting remains of the Monastery of St Euthymius can still be seen, but only after a 3 kilometre cross-country trek due south from the same kilometrestone 15 which led you to Ein Fara.

Back on the main road, you notice the Inn of the Good Samaritan, scene of the New Testament tale related in the gospel of St Luke, of a 'certain man who went down from Jerusalem to Jericho and fell among thieves'. From time immemorial this has been a caravanserai on the way from Jerusalem to Jericho and the east, an inn on the pilgrim route

The Inn of the Good Samaritan near Ma'ale Adummim

between the two biblical cities and a strategic point of great military value.

Referred to as Ma'ale Adummim ('Red Pass') in Joshua 15:7, its name derives partly from the colour of its soil and partly from the blood so often spilled by the robbers infesting the area. Written evidence proves that here was an inn during Second Temple times, while centuries later the Byzantine Monastery of St Joachim arose on the same site. During the Middle Ages, the Crusaders erected their Castle of Maldoim on the hill above to protect the pilgrim road, and you can still see the barrel-vaulted halls, deep moat and water cisterns of the Crusader knights. The present structure by the side of the road was a Turkish police post.

About 4 kilometres beyond Ma'ale Adummim, a poorly surfaced path to the left will take you over some 10 bumpy kilometres to the Greek-Orthodox Monastery of St George of Coziba near the mouth of Wadi Kelt, not far from Jericho. Among the few Judean Desert monasteries still functioning, this curious building, which seems to cling to the almost perpendicular mountain slope, is called by the Arabs Deir Mar Jarris ('the House of Father George'). Steep steps lead up to a gold-and-black door, through which you ascend another flight to the monks' quarters and yet another to a small, dimly lit chapel crammed with icons, paintings and hanging lamps. On the floor your monk guide will point out a Shield of David, said to remain from a 4th-century AD synagogue above which Justinian built a church in 530.

The monastery is named for an early Christian saint, George (or Georgios), who lived in the nearby Monastery of Coziba, then became a hermit in a cave in Wadi Kelt. Gradually, other anchorites gathered around him, and he founded a Laura which was destroyed in AD 614. Rebuilt by the Crusaders, it became known as the Monastery of St George of Coziba. The site was later abandoned, and only in 1880 did the present Deir Mar Jarris arise on the same spot.

Five kilometres past the turning to Deir Mar Jarris a signpost indicates 'To Nebi Musa'. It lies barely a kilometre off the road, on an easily negotiable track, and according to Moslem folklore it is the sanctuary where Moses is buried. Appearing with magical suddenness upon the barren, form-

The Monastery of St George in Wadi Kelt

less landscape, the compound, with its high walls, minarets and rows of squat domes, has a strange and unearthly quality.

A colossal stone cenotaph marks the grave of Moses, who is venerated by Moslems as well as Jews. Around this cenotaph the Mameluke sultan Baybars, conqueror of the Crusaders, erected a mosque and initiated a Moslem pilgrimage to neutralize the Christian pilgrim throngs. On the Friday of Easter Week, Moslems would congregate outside the el-Aqsa Mosque and march to Nebi Musa, attacking Christians coming up to celebrate Easter in Jerusalem; then they would

Nebi Musa

spend five festive days in the courtyards of the mosque before returning home.

At the beginning of the British Mandate, when the religion of the ruling power became Christian instead of Moslem, the Moslem spring festival took on an anti-Jewish aspect. Mobs of Palestinian Arabs chanting anti-Jewish slogans would incite the crowds to riot. After the 1948 War of Independence, Jordan cancelled the Nebi Musa ceremonies, for they had become an exclusively Palestinian Arab affair, and the authorities feared a division in the readjusting nation.

Jericho

Thought to be the oldest city in the world, Jericho is barely 40 kilometres south-east of Jerusalem. Already a walled town with a long history when Joshua crossed the Jordan, the Jericho of today is a townlet of some 7,000 inhabitants, sweltering in the hot, humid atmosphere of 250 metres below sea level. Flame-flowered poincianas line the streets; date palms, bananas, mangoes (rather unfairly known as 'ugly fruit'), pomelos and other exotic fruits grow in tropical profusion, for together with the extreme heat, Jericho is rich in water and could readily become the paradise it was when Herod reigned and Cleopatra's balsam gardens were in full bloom.

Jericho

Jericho's present citizens, darker complexioned than the majority of Arabs, are finding life not too easy, for most of the hotels which used to cater for winter vacations have fallen on difficult days, although restaurants and gift shops catering for the crowds of tourists are doing well. However, with more effective use of the water resources in the vicinity, agriculture is improving and the fields and orchards are yielding far better crops than before. Stalls of vegetables and shining oranges and clementinas, picked with their dark-green leaves, make an attractive picture; and when they are not otherwise occupied, the Jericho menfolk sit around in open-air cafés smoking *narghilas* (Oriental water-pipes) and drinking syrupy black coffee.

Over the ages, Jericho has altered its location only within

The round tower at Jericho

narrow limits, staying close to Elisha's Spring, or Ein es-Sultan, adjoining Tel es-Sultan with the 8000 BC settlement excavated by Dr Kathleen Kenyon. Its monumental round tower, 10 metres across, with a very steep internal stairway rising from ground level to an aperture at the top, speaks well for the skill and craftsmanship of the people of those far-off days. As yet the single example of this type of construction ever found, it marks the first step taken by man from nomadic to permanent living.

Beginning in 1868, four digs were made on this fascinating site,

The Monastery of Karantel

and early finds included the nine-thousand-year-old plastered skulls decorated with shell 'eyes' and white stone 'teeth'. Dr Kenyon's work, begun in 1952, revealed layer after layer of settlement, abandonment and resettlement for thousands of years. A big gap occurred in the fourth millennium BC – the Chalcolithic or Copper Age; then people of a higher civilization reappeared near Ein es-Sultan, building houses and burying their dead in rock tombs, examples of which can be seen in the Rockefeller Museum, Jerusalem.

It was one of these flourishing walled towns which fell to the blast of Joshua's trumpets around 1250 BC, and although Joshua forbade the rebuilding of the conquered city, I Kings tells how Hiel the Bethelite restored it early in the 9th century BC– a restoration which lasted for four hundred years.

The Book of the Maccabees relates that Simon made Ptolemy, his Egyptian son-in-law, governor of the district of Jericho and then, together with his sons Judas and Mattathias, paid him an official visit in 135 BC. Ptolemy entertained them in his hilltop castle of Duk, above the spring Ein Duk, and the present-day Monastery of Karantel. Hoping to usurp the throne, 'Ptolemee and his men rose up and took their weapons, and came upon Simon into the banqueting place, and slew him and his two sons'.

Karantel, a Greek-Orthodox monastery, is the traditional place of Jesus' forty days of fasting in order to resist the devil's tempting offer to give him all the kingdoms of the world 'if thou wilt worship me'. Jesus' final answer was 'It is written, Thou shalt worship the Lord thy God, and Him only shalt thou serve'.

Herod rebuilt Jericho further south across Wadi Kelt. Utilizing Wadi Kelt's rich springs, he erected an elaborate system of aqueducts, some of them still in use, and planted dates, myrrh and balsam which fetched high prices in the markets of Greece and Rome. Here he built his winter palace and the fortress of Cypros, named for his mother. It was in the pool attached to this palace that Herod drowned his handsome young brother-in-law, Mariamne's brother Aristobolus, whom he feared as a possible rival to the throne.

Jericho continued to thrive under the Romans, and there was a Jewish settlement in it even after the fall of Jerusalem. The Christian population gradually increased – in Byzantine days it had its own bishopric – while the Jews concentrated in the hamlet of Na'aran to the north.

An early 7th-century AD mosaic synagogue floor, discovered in 1936 beneath one of the Jericho houses, can be seen on payment of a small entrance fee. In the centre is the famous medallion with a *menora,* palm branch *(lulav),* and ram's horn *(shofar)* and a Hebrew inscription, 'Peace upon Israel'.

Another ancient synagogue – this one from the 6th century – can be seen at nearby Nueima, the fertile oasis created by the springs of Ein Duk and Ein Nueima, which was in Talmudic times the Jewish town of Na'aran. Today a swimming pool fed by the springs and a pleasant tree-shaded café enable you to spend a refreshing half-hour before trudging up to the hill-top remains of the synagogue. Ask the café owner for the key to the protective fence.

Revealed by a chance shell fired at British troops from Austrian gun positions during World War One, the synagogue was excavated in 1921 by a team from the French School of Biblical Archaeology. They cleared the zodiac wheel with its Hebrew writing, the bird, animal and fruit motifs and the intricate patterned borders. Most of the human figures had been defaced, possibly by the Arabs who invaded this area in AD 638, possibly by ultra-orthodox Jews who took very seriously the injunction 'Thou shalt not make unto thee any graven image'.

Of the mosaic commemorative inscriptions written in Aramaic, most striking was that set into the main entry above a beautifully designed *menora*. Removed for safe keeping, it has now vanished without a trace. Other inscriptions from the synagogue of Na'aran are in the Rockefeller Museum and in the headquarters of the School of Biblical Archaeology at St Stephen's in Jerusalem.

Not far away from Nueima – in fact, an aqueduct from the Nueima spring once supplied it with water – is Khirbet Mafjar, the Winter Palace of Caliph Hisham ibn Abd el-Malik. One of the finest examples of 8th-century Arab architecture, it has an entrance hall with niches for statues; a pillared courtyard with a stone tracery window, formerly part of the upper storey, standing in the centre; two mosques and a small and a large bath house with tesserated floors and elaborate heating systems.

Most impressive is the room known as the Guest Chamber. Lined by stone benches and paved with geometrically designed mosaic flooring, it has a raised dais at one end with an exquisite design of a lion attacking one of three fawns nibbling at the leaves of a dark-green tree. Made of tiny coloured stone cubes, it is a perfect specimen of a mosaic carpet.

above *Ruin from Hisham's Palace*

opposite *The aqueduct from the Nueima spring*

Excavated in 1936, Khirbet Mafjar was found to include columns from a Byzantine church, as well as quantities of lively
painted stucco figures of animals and people. Chiselled tablets unearthed indicate that Caliph Hisham began to build
a modest hunting lodge here around AD 724, but the plan
became more and more ambitious, and by the time its completion was taken over by his nephew, Walid II , it had a forecourt, a great bath house, the second mosque and a
compound which enclosed several square kilometres of
parkland as a private game reserve. Completed in 743, its
owners enjoyed their luxurious estate for but a few years, for
the earthquake of 747 damaged it beyond repair.

Khirbet Qumran

On the shores of the Dead Sea, Khirbet Qumran, some 10 kilometres south of Jericho, has proved to be one of the wonders of the modern world. Lying between the seashore and the bleak, cave-pitted cliffs behind, these heaps of ruins had never aroused more than the usual interest in archaeological sites until 1947, when two Bedouin shepherd boys looking for a stray goat found seven of the tall, now-familiar earthenware jars in a cave high up in the hill. Inside the jars were parchment fragments and disintegrating scrolls – manuscripts that were to unlock a whole new world to biblical scholars.

Illiterate as they were, the boys realized that this was something special, and took their finds back to the Bedouin camp. Eventually the scrolls reached a Syrian-Christian merchant in Bethlehem, who showed his acquisition to the Metropolitan of the Assyrian Church of St Mark in the Old City. After a year's delay, the Metropolitan brought the scrolls to the American School of Oriental Research in Jerusalem for evaluation.

Meanwhile, Professor E. L. Sukenik, head of the Department of Archaeology at the Hebrew University, had managed to obtain some of this remarkable material despite the uneasy conditions immediately preceding the 1948 Israeli-Arab war. All these events triggered off a series of frenzied searches of all the caves in the Qumran area, of buying and selling of scrolls and even scraps of parchment and of worldwide contacts between scholars trying to interpret these remarkable finds.

The task of scientifically excavating Khirbet Qumran was undertaken by Father Roland de Vaux and Lancaster Harding, who began their dig in 1951, exposing a complete settlement of the strange monastic sect, the Essenes. Here they lived and worked from some time in the 2nd century BC (the Hasmonean era) until the fall of Jerusalem. You can still see in the main building the entrance tower, kitchen, laundry, a capacious cistern, a ritual bath and the all-important scriptorium where the members copied the already ancient manuscripts.

An adjacent wing holds an Assembly Hall, probably also a refectory, where all the community ate together, for in a side chamber opening off the main hall were sherds of more than a thousand plates, dishes and bowls for the members' meals. This wing also included a complete potter's workshop with a large kiln, a number of cisterns and other ritual baths supplied by a complex system of water conduits. Between the compound and the Dead Sea was the communal graveyard, also excavated by Father de Vaux's team.

Who were these people, whose life and actions of over two thousand years ago are so strongly affecting the thinking of today? They were the Essenes, derived from the Hebrew Hasidim ('The Righteous Ones'), who, tiring of the pomp and ceremony of Temple observances, journeyed east across the Judean Desert as refugees and seekers of solitude have done down the ages. Here, at the mouth of Wadi Qumran, on the long-abandoned ruins of the fortified 'city of Salt' (Joshua 15:62), they made their homes.

Leading a communal, monastic life, carrying out the accepted rites in their own way and stressing the aspect of personal cleanliness, the Essenes, according to Josephus, 'have all things in common, so that a rich man enjoys no more of his own wealth than he who hath nothing. There are about 4,000 men that live in this way, and neither marry wives nor are desirous to keep servants'.

Josephus also discourses at length about their habits and customs and how they 'take great pains in studying the writings of the ancients'. Inspired by these studies, the Qumran scribes wrote countless copies, and the documents already found include the Scroll of Isaiah (now exhibited in the Shrine of the Book in Jerusalem), Ecclesiastes, the Pentateuch, the War of the Sons of Light against the Sons of Darkness, the Essenes Manual of Discipline, the Habakkuk Commentary and many others.

Two of the best known are the Copper Scroll, recording places where the Temple treasure was hidden at the approach of the Romans, and the Temple Scroll, acquired by Professor

Qumran

Yadin (former archaeologist-soldier son of Prof. Sukenik) after the Six Day War.

Archaeological evidence revealed that from the 31 BC earthquake until about 4 BC – practically for the whole of Herod the Great's reign – Qumran was abandoned. It revived in the early days of the Christian era and flourished until it was attacked and razed by Roman troops in AD 68.

How did the monks manage to save this precious heritage? Apparently the custom was to store all manuscripts in earthenware jars made in the settlement's pottery workshop and to keep them in the neighbouring caves, where they were protected by the dry, even atmosphere yet easily available if required. When the Roman soldiers drew near, other scrolls and parchments were hurriedly packed into the cave store-

Ein Feshka

rooms, to be discovered only after two thousand years.

Nearby Ein Feshka, with its fresh-water springs, was the agricultural hub of the Qumran settlement. On excavation, canals for the distribution of water to the fields were found, as well as byres for sheep, goats and cattle. What appears to have been a tannery was also discovered.

Today, the springs of Ein Feshka form a favourite recreation centre, particularly for excursionists from Jerusalem, which is barely three-quarters of an hour away. Here you can bathe in the warm, salt-saturated waters of the lowest lake in the world – 400 metres below sea level – have a refreshing sweet-water shower or a dip in the swimming pool, then fill up with coffee or a light meal before making the return journey to your hotel.

The Jordan Valley

An amazing engineering feat completed over the past few years was the laying of the highway along the Jordan Valley. Running from Beit Shean to Jericho, roughly parallel to the winding river bed, it passes through bare but potentially fertile soil, for hitherto untapped ground water has been found in the vicinity. To the north it connects with the road to Tiberias, Galilee and the Golan Heights, while to the south it hugs the Dead Sea coastline, passes Ein Gedi, Sodom and the Arava to Eilat, then joins the recently finished road edging the eastern shore of the Sinai Peninsula to Sharm el-Sheikh.

Around this area and along the new highway are a number of Nahal (Pioneering Fighting Youth) settlements, manned by eighteen- to twenty-one-year-old youngsters who combine their pioneering work with their army service. The sensitive boundary must be patrolled and protected, and to this end a number of Nahal outposts have been set up. Strangely enough, this line generally conforms to the defence line of Hasmonean and Herodian fortresses of over two thousand years ago.

Southernmost is Mitzpe Shalem, named for one of this area's early pioneers. It is located 600 metres above the level of the Dead Sea on a bleak hill-top called by the Arabs Ras Turba, from the Turba spring issuing from its depths. If you take the steep, winding road up to the summit, you will be rewarded by a magnificent view over the whole of the Dead Sea and across to Jordan.

Then comes Nahal Kallia, directly south of Jericho on the northern shore of the Dead Sea, where a nearby restaurant faintly echoes the pre-1948 Kallia Hotel. Next is Nahal Na'aran, north of Jericho and close to the ancient synagogue of the same name, and Nahal Gilgal, recalling the Israelites' first encampment after crossing the Jordan into the Promised Land.

At the foot of Mount Sartaba is Nahal Masua ('Beacon'), a reminder that, in Second Temple days, Sartaba was one of the

Beacon Hills. The appearance of the new moon was signalled by the Temple priests lighting flares or beacons on the Mount of Olives. Then these would be seen by watchers on Sartaba and relayed further to the rest of the country. Masua's young people have revived the custom by climbing to the summit on the first day of Hanukkah and kindling beacons seen far and wide.

Continuing northwards along the Jordan Valley are two new Nahal outposts – Nahal Argaman and Nahal Mehola at the edge of Mount Gilboa. Nahal Argaman is not far from the Damiya Bridge, one of the three bridges spanning the southern part of the Jordan River. It was here, close to the biblical city of Adam, that Joshua watched while 'all the Israelites passed over on dry ground . . . clean over Jordan'. Presumably there was a shallow ford here in ancient times, as there was at the site of other bridges across the river.

Damiya Bridge is the link between Samaria and Amman; Allenby Bridge, just to the south – the only one presently in use – connects Jericho to the Jordanian capital, while Abdullah Bridge, named for Jordan's first ruler, is almost equi-distant between Jerusalem and Amman, which are barely 85 kilometres apart. For security reasons, all three were blown up by Israeli forces in June 1967, and the Damiya and Allenby bridges were replaced by temporary structures.

Allenby Bridge is today the accepted and well-controlled crossing through which thousands of Arabs journey to and from Israel for family reunions and business and holiday visits, while in accordance with the 'Open Bridges' policy of Israel's government, trucks and other vehicles pass daily with loads of fruits, vegetables and other commodities.

Grouped directly north of the Abdullah Bridge, where the Jordan drops into the Dead Sea, are a number of Christian shrines commemorating the place of the Baptism of Jesus by John. Best known is the Greek-Orthodox Monastery of St John, called by the Arabs Qasr el-Yahud ('Castle of the Jews') from the tradition that at this shallow ford Joshua led his people over the river and into the Land of Canaan.

Originally built in the 4th century AD, the Monastery of St

The new road along the Dead Sea

John is located 356 metres below sea level and is the lowest-lying monastery in the world. It is also, at least for the moment, the only one of the baptismal shrines still accessible, for to reach those of the other denominations – the Abyssinian, Armenian, Coptic, Franciscan, Rumanian and Syrian, for example – you must apply for a pass to the Israel Defence Forces headquarters.

The Road to Bethlehem

Kibbutz Ramat Rachel, reached by branching off the road to Bethlehem, was founded in 1926 but destroyed during the Arab riots of 1929. Resettled, it was again attacked and changed hands several times during the 1948 War of Independence, then was revived once more in 1950. Before the Six Day War, Ramat Rachel was on Jerusalem's southernmost tip, and from the kibbutz watertower you could look over into Jordanian territory at the spires of Bethlehem; at the village of Tekoa, birthplace of Amos the prophet; and at Beit Jala, or Beit Giloh, home of David's advisor Ahitophel, who, 'when he saw that his counsel was not followed, gat him home . . . put his household in order, and hanged himself'.

This vantage point was a favourite stop for tourists, who are now hurried on and not given the opportunity to see the Ramat Rachel excavations of a 7th-century BC palace of the First Temple period accidentally discovered when the watertower was built. Great capitals like those found in the palaces of Hazor and Megiddo were found here, too, as well as massive foundations, walls, and distinctive red-painted, carved window balustrades, indicating the richness of the building.

Who was the king of Judah who lived here, away from his own capital, 2,600 years ago? Some think it was King Uzziah, who became a leper and 'dwelt in a several house', but he reigned from 780 to 740 BC, rather too early to conform with archaeological data. More acceptable is the theory that it was wicked King Jehoiakim, who ruled from 608 to 598 BC. Jehoiakim was unpopular with his people, and Jeremiah the prophet accused him of using his neighbour's services without wages to 'build a wide house . . . ceiled with cedar, and painted with vermilion', like the painted balustrades found here.

Ramat Rachel, then known as Kathismus ('The Seat'), was traditionally one of the places where Mary and Joseph rested on their journey to Bethlehem, and the remains of a Byzantine commemorative monastery, with mosaics and

Mar Elias

wine presses, can be seen above the ruins of the palace.

Back on the main road to Bethlehem, you soon see the romantic-looking Greek-Orthodox Monastery of Mar Elias, first built during the 6th century on the spot where the Prophet Elijah is said to have slept on his flight from Queen Jezebel's wrath. Rebuilt in 1160 after one of the severe earthquakes which periodically cause damage in the Holy Land, it has since been in constant use.

Strategically placed on a hillock 800 metres above sea level, with an uninterrupted view across to Jerusalem on the north and to Bethlehem on the south, Mar Elias was an important border point during the 1948–67 period. Underground gun emplacements honeycombed the adjoining slopes, now happily only a reminder of nineteen uneasy years.

Opposite the monastery is a memorial to an Israeli Air Force pilot who fell in action in June 1967, and close by is another in the form of a stone bench inscribed with verses from the Bible in Hebrew, English, Arabic and Greek. This bench, put up by his wife Edith, commemorates the English Victorian artist William Holman Hunt, who lived in Palestine for many years while he painted his famous biblical pictures, including the huge canvas 'The Light of the World', in St Paul's Cathedral, London.

Directly on the road is the impressive entrance to the compound called Tantour, belonging to the Austrian Order of the Knights of Malta. Originally planned to provide medical services for the local population, it was opened in 1876 but somehow never succeeded. After changing hands several times, it has now been reorganized as the Ecumenical Institute for Advanced Theological Studies, with about forty students from all over the world. The Rockefeller Foundation has provided a maintenance fund, and a Jewish family from Chicago the money for its library.

The small domed structure called Rachel's Tomb marks the grave of Jacob's favourite wife. The book of Genesis tells how she died while giving birth to Benjamin, her younger son, and 'was buried in the way to Ephrath, which is Bethlehem. Jacob set a pillar upon her grave: that is the pillar of Rachel's grave unto this day'.

Revered by Christians and Moslems as well as Jews, this time-honoured shrine has been accepted for centuries. Mentioned by the Bordeaux Pilgrim in AD 333, then noted by later pilgrims as being surmounted by a pyramid of stones, it was rebuilt by the Crusaders, who protected the cenotaph by a high-domed roof supported by four columns. So it remained until 1788, when the arches were blocked to form a closed chamber. In 1841 Sir Moses Montefiore managed to persuade the Turkish government to transfer the property to Jewish ownership, and he himself had the building repaired and added a vestibule with a *mihrab* for Moslem worship.

Except for the gap between 1948 and 1967, when the Jordanians forbade access to the Jews, Rachel's Tomb has

Rachel's Tomb

been a popular place for Jewish pilgrimage. Until today streams of pilgrims, particularly women, come to pray (especially for fertility and male offspring) at the grave of the famous matriarch of Israel, and to tuck petitions into the crevices in the wall behind the towering stone cenotaph.

This entire area is rich in biblical history. Along this way, four thousand years ago, journeyed the nomad Patriarchs, constantly on the move, constantly in search of water, constantly seeking good pasture for their flocks. Even before the coming of Abraham and his family, when 'Abel was a keeper of sheep', Bethlehem was a good pastoral centre, for its encircling valleys and caves affording shelter to man and beast provided ideal conditions. A look-out tower might well have been built here to keep an eye on straying flocks, and indeed, after Jacob buried Rachel, he 'journeyed and spread his tent beyond the tower of Edar'.

These idyllic surroundings saw the drama of the book of

Ruth, the lovely Moabite widow who accompanied her mother-in-law, Naomi, back 'to Bethlehem in the beginning of barley harvest'. Here she married Boaz, her wealthy kinsman, and became the great-grandmother of King David. It was here, too, that the prophet Samuel sought the young David 'who keepeth the sheep'. A thousand years later, yet another miracle is ascribed to this same place, for shepherds 'abiding in the field keeping watch over their flock by night', were told by angels of Jesus' birth.

During Byzantine days, monasteries and chapels dotted the hills around. Khirbet Mahrum, Khirbet el-Kait, Khirbet Juhza are but a few places where you can still notice the remains of buildings and mosaic pavements of that time. One of them, called the Shepherd's Field, has now been rebuilt as the Latin Chapel of the Franciscan fathers. A tent-shaped prayer hall, designed by Antonio Barluzzi, with beautiful interior decorations, it is located a little east of Bethlehem. It stands upon the ruins of a Byzantine church – the Church of the Holy Shepherd – and of an agricultural homestead from Herodian times.

As recently as Christmas 1972, one of these ruins known as Kenisat Errauat ('Church of the Shepherds') was excavated, and a fine 6th-century Byzantine church, with mosaic pavements, was discovered. In the crypt more than 100 skeletons were found, as well as coins, vessels and oil lamps from the same time. The Greek-Orthodox Patriarchate, who own the site, intend building a new church there.

Beit Jala, on the outskirts of Bethlehem, is thought to be the biblical Giloh, Ahitophel's home town. A Christian Arab townlet of about 10,000 people, it stands nearly 1,000 metres above sea level. Its breeze-catching height has made it a favourite summer resort for residents of Judea and Samaria. There are also a number of Christian institutions there – churches, convents and schools – and if you feel energetic, you can walk across the hills for some 3 kilometres to the Cremisan Monastery, with its famous winery and vineyards. From the hill summit a wonderful view opens out over New Jerusalem, and this commanding site made an ideal stance for the guns which shelled Jerusalem's southern suburbs during the Six Day War. This installation is now an agricultural field-school.

Herodion

'Three score furlongs distant from Jerusalem is the citadel of Herodion', wrote Josephus Flavius nearly two thousand years ago. Since then it has stood, tall and challenging, one of a line of defence fortresses along the western shore of the Dead Sea, protecting Palestine against enemy incursions from the east. South of Herodion is famed Massada; north of it the bastions of Hyrcania, Cypros and Sartaba, sometimes called Alexandrion after the Hasmonean king Alexander Jannaeus.

Easily reached by taking a clearly marked road to the left just before you enter Bethlehem, Herodion is 800 metres above sea level, but is not difficult of access, as it rises but 100 metres or so above the plateau. Even in its present state, this mighty citadel bears a remarkable resemblance to Josephus' description, for he recorded that Herod built a fortress upon a mountain, and 'built round towers all about the top of it, and filled up the remaining space with costly palaces'. Josephus continued, 'he brought a mighty quantity of water from a great distance, and raised an ascent to it of two hundred steps of the whitest marble'. All of this is archaeologically true, for signs have been found of an aqueduct from the springs of Artas near Solomon's Pools to the cisterns at the foot of the hill, where traces of the 'steps of whitest marble' have also been discovered.

As for the 'round towers', their bases are clearly marked. There were four – to the north, west, south and east – and of these, the completely circular east tower was largest and strongest, while the other three projected from the circular line of the wall, providing protection on all sides. The approach road from the bottom of the hill continues between the double walls, and within the deep cone formed by the walls and towers are the remains of Herod's palatial halls, with mosaic floors and coloured frescoes.

Two of the most striking structures within the cone are the elaborate bath house and the synagogue, with a double row of columns and stone benches lining three of the walls. Just outside the synagogue is a stepped ritual bath, and one of the side chambers is piled with stone balls some 30 centimetres in diameter – ammunition for the catapult machines fired in unsuccessful attempts to drive away the Roman troops. Recent excavations have confirmed the existence of tremendous underground cisterns first noted in 1880 and have revealed a wide gate leading through a concealed passage into the centre of the compound.

Herodion, built by Herod soon after his ascension to power in 37 BC, was intended to be a defence point, a pleasure palace for himself and his friends during his lifetime and a regal mausoleum for him after his death. He died in Jericho in 4 BC, and Josephus Flavius reports of Herod's funeral that 'There was a bier of all gold, embroidered with precious stones . . . a diadem was put upon his head, and a crown of gold above it . . . and the body was carried to Herodion'.

This stronghold became a bastion against the Romans, hold-

Herodion

ing out for two years after the fall of Jerusalem; then it fulfilled the same purpose during Bar-Kokhba's rebellion, for some of the Bar-Kokhba letters found in Wadi Murabat in 1954 mention Herodion as one of the rebel outposts.

Since then, except for the Byzantine hermits who lived among the ruins, Herodion has been deserted. During the recent past, many hitherto unknown details have come to light, and since the Six Day War much work has been done there. However, Herodion's closely guarded secret – the royal tomb of Herod, with its riches, gold and precious stones – is still as shrouded in mystery as ever.

Stone 'cannon balls' at Herodion

Bethlehem

Bethlehem, barely 10 kilometres south of Jerusalem, has a magic of its own. A quiet and friendly township on a hill ridge 800 metres above sea level, it seems to have absorbed something of its tranquil past. One of the all-too-few places in the Holy Land associated almost entirely with peaceful events, its link with the Jewish people begins nearly four thousand years ago, when Jacob, sojourning through Bethlehem, lost his young wife, Rachel, in childbirth.

View of Bethlehem

The Church of the Nativity

Bethlehem of today has a population of around 32,000, mainly Christian Arabs. With professions geared, as in the past, to serving pilgrims of all kinds, they are skilled gold-smiths and adept in carving exquisite mother-of-pearl articles and olivewood figures with religious motifs. Shops for souvenirs abound, as well as small cafés and general stores, but the single lodestar attracting every visitor is the Basilica of the Nativity.

Traditional birth-place of Jesus, where Mary gave birth to her infant, 'and laid him in a manger; because there was no room for them in the inn', the Church of the Nativity is one of the holiest shrines in Christendom. In front of the church, a spacious flagged courtyard leads up to the stone façade where, if you look carefully, you can see the broad, straight Byzantine lintel above the present doorway. Below it, the pointed-arched Crusader entry made the opening smaller and more defensible, while it was cut down even further – also for security reasons – during Turkish times.

Stooping through a low aperture, you reach a vestibule, then enter the basilica by way of a huge wooden door. Almost unchanged since its erection by Emperor Justinian in the 6th century AD the church has four rows of twelve tall, red-brown marble pillars forming a nave and double side aisles.

The two end pillars in each row are cut off by some later construction, and faded paintings on the lower part of the pillars were added by pilgrims. Above them are Crusader portraits of saints from the East and the West, with their names written in Greek lettering, while above the pillars, on the walls, the Crusaders also added fine glass mosaics, now sadly damaged.

A massive, pink-marble font stands on the right in the south aisle, while trapdoors in the nave cover sections of a sixteen-hundred-year-old church built by Constantine (disclosed in 1933). At the further end of the nave, above the Grotto of the Nativity, rises a platform, originally the hexagonal altar of the 4th century structure. Around the platform are three transepts, richly ornamented with lamps, screens and tapestries, which were built on by Justinian. Narrow steps descend to the Grotto of the Nativity, where an alcove marked by a silver star is generally accepted as the birth-place of Jesus, while a rock-cut trough in a side cavern is said to be the manger where he was cradled.

A side door from the main church opens into the secluded forecourt of the Franciscan Chapel of St Catherine, beautifully restored in 1949 by Antonio Barluzzi, who incorporated much of the original masonry. In the centre of the quadrangle stands a statue of 4th-century St Jerome, who, with the help of Jewish scholars, translated the Bible into Latin. Called the Vulgate Bible, it made the Holy

overleaf *The Grotto of the Nativity*

Book familiar to a far wider range of people and is still the official version used by the Roman Catholic Church. From St Catherine's Chapel you descend to a labyrinth of rock-hewn graves. Interlinking one with the other, these subterranean chambers lead through to the Grotto of the Nativity, although the separating door is now kept permanently closed.

Local tradition – an important factor in establishing the location of all the holy shrines – pointed out the grotto of Jesus' birth at the very beginning of the Christian era. Thus, when Emperor Constantine laid the foundations of his basilica, there was no hesitation in choosing the site. A hole was pierced in the rock roof of the grotto and an octagonal structure raised upon it. The basilica itself, large and splendid, extended westward from the sanctuary, where the present church stands.

Two hundred years later there was a violent Samaritan uprising, which resulted in terrible damage to Christian institutions and a high death toll among the rebels. Emperor Justinian rebuilt the church soon afterwards, very much as you see it now, and added a mosaic picture of the Three Wise Men on the pediment above the entry. The church was unharmed by the ravaging Persian hordes in AD 614 – possibly spared because the pictured Magi wore Persian dress!

Although the Crusaders made many decorative additions and built on St Catherine's Chapel, they made no structural changes in the basilica. During this medieval era, Bethlehem was a wealthy, thriving pilgrim centre, but with the fall of the Crusader Kingdom of Jerusalem, its good fortune ceased and it became a bone of contention between various factions of the Christian church.

Today the main ownership is shared between the Greek Orthodox, the Armenians and the Franciscans, while the Copts, Syrians and Protestants have certain rights of worship. Christmas is celebrated three times a year – the Western Christmas from the night of the 24th through 25th December; the Eastern Christmas from the night of the 6th through the 7th January; and the Armenian Christmas from the night of the 18th through the 19th January.

The Road to Hebron

Continuing for about 3 kilometres south along the road to Hebron, you see on your right an arched gateway with a bas-relief of St George killing the dragon. This gateway leads into the village of el-Khadr – the Arabic name for St George – where there is little of interest except the Greek-Orthodox Church and monastery, once an asylum for the insane and where the chains shackling the unfortunate patients can still be seen in the cellars. However, this is the easiest way to Battir, a prosperous Arab village which grew up on the site of ancient Betar, where Shimon Bar-Kokhba and his followers made their last stand against the Romans.

After Jerusalem fell to Titus in AD 70 there were sixty years of an uneasy truce between mighty Rome and tiny, valiant Judea. Tension gradually mounted until in AD 132 Bar-Kokhba's revolt broke out, and for three years Jerusalem was again independent. This last spark of freedom was short-lived. The Romans rallied their forces and in AD 135 brought strong reinforcements to fight little Judea. They drove Bar-Kokhba from Jerusalem, then from one mountain fortress after another until he concentrated his remaining strength here in Betar, 8 kilometres south-west of the capital.

Surrounding the hillock, the Roman Army set itself up for a long siege, building camps and earth ramparts ready for the final attack. Betar was conquered, and with it died the final flicker of Jewish independence for nearly two thousand years. The Romans, ired by the persistence and tenacity of their opponents, carried out one of the cruellest massacres in the whole of their cruel history. The handful of survivors were sold into slavery in the market-place at Ramat el-Khalil near Hebron, and darkness shrouded Judea and Jerusalem for generations.

Battir is today a thriving agricultural settlement close to the Jerusalem–Tel Aviv railway line. Its communal life is centred around the rich spring, still used for irrigation and for domestic chores. On either side of the water outlet were

Latin inscriptions (now almost illegible) recalling the two Roman legions – the 5th Macedonians and the 11th Claudian – encamped here during the ill-fated siege. You can see the deep rock-cut conduit which distributed the spring water to the plantations, while towering above the source is the huge, brooding mound of Betar, known to the Arabs as Khirbet el-Yahud ('Ruin of the Jews').

Tradition dies hard in the Holy Land, and although none of the local residents can tell you why the mound is so called, the name Khirbet el-Yahud has clung to this particular spot for nearly twenty centuries – a silent memorial to the martyrdom of Shimon Bar-Kokhba and his heroic band.

Another kilometre along the main road brings you to King Solomon's Pools in fertile, spring-fed Wadi Tahunat. Guarded by Qalat el-Burak ('Castle of the Pools'), erected some five hundred years ago, and ringed by a well-grown pine forest, these three great open reservoirs form a green and lovely park, ideal for picnics and recreation.

'I made me gardens and orchards, and I planted trees . . . I made me pools of water', declared Solomon in Ecclesiastes (2:4–5), and tradition holds that here were his orchards and these his pools. Partly masonry-built, partly hewn from the rock, the upper pool is about 120 by 70 metres and has a capacity of about 45,000 cubic metres. The middle pool, edged by wide, white rock-shelves, holds about the same, while the enormous lower pool takes nearly four times as much.

Water has always been a problem for Jerusalem. With no river or sweet-water lake in the vicinity, and with rains falling only in the winter months, the city depended on springs such as the Gihon (in the Kidron Valley) and on the conservation of rainfall, which is quite high (averaging between 500 and 600 millimetres annually, little less than that of London, Paris or Berlin, but concentrated in only four to five months.

David's Jerusalem managed quite well with the Gihon, but as the town grew, it needed more and more water. Huge cisterns were constructed in the Temple enclosure; others, such as the Pool of Mamilla and the Sultan's Pool, in the valleys; and still others, like the Pool of Israel, against a retaining wall.

Solomon's Pools

They were plaster lined to prevent seepage and were normally filled during the rainy season.

Aqueducts were made, utilizing sources further afield, like the springs of Wadi Tahunat and those of Wadi Arrub, 8 kilometres to the south. There was a high-level and a low-level aqueduct to Jerusalem, the latter originating from Solomon's Pools and reaching the Temple cisterns by way of Mount Zion and Wilson's Viaduct, while the straighter, more efficient high-level aqueduct drew water into the Mamilla Pool and thence into Hezekiah's Pool in the Old City.

Under Herodian rule, both aqueducts to Jerusalem were kept in order – the high-level one making use of the upper-most of the three Pools of Solomon, and the low-level one fed from the middle and lower pools. Another Herodian water conduit ran from Artas, the pretty village at the foot of the pools, to the cisterns of Herod's fortress of Herodion. After AD 70, when the city's population dropped from around a quarter of a million to far, far less – mostly living around the Upper City – the high-level aqueduct was cared for, as it supplied this part of Jerusalem, while the low-level one fell into disrepair.

Restored and neglected over and over again, according to the government of the time, the aqueducts were found to be inadequate for modern needs when the British took over in 1918. They began to pump in water from the low-lying springs to the east; to clean and refill the cisterns in private homes and courtyards; and in 1936 they brought up water from the plain – from Rosh Ha'ayin, the sources of the Yarkon River.

Pipelines from the south, east and west were disrupted by the 1948 war, and Jerusalem under siege had to rely on its scanty emergency stores. Fortunately, this critical period was soon over, and normal conditions were restored, while the discovery of huge underground lakes stretching west of the capital have eased the situation in a miraculous fashion.

To reach the religious settlement of Kfar Etzion you must branch right off the main highway at kilometrestone 20 about 7 kilometres past King Solomon's Pools. Kfar Etzion, reborn since the Six Day War, was originally founded in this overwhelmingly Arab section of the country in 1927, when it was called Migdal Edar. The first settlers were obliged to leave in 1929, when Arab rioting became a very real danger, but sixteen years after the withdrawal Kfar Etzion was re-established at a lovely spot close by, nearly 1,000 metres above sea level. Masuot Itzhak, its neighbour, was settled in 1946; Ein Zurim a year later; and Revadim, the single non-religious group, in 1947, forming what was called the Etzion Bloc.

Arab antagonism was strong and flared up even more strongly with the United Nations' decision on partition, for the U.N. borders of Jewish Palestine did not include the Etzion Bloc. The road between it and Jerusalem was in Arab hands. Communications and supplies were cut, and a company of thirty-five Palmach soldiers who set out as a relief party to the besieged settlements was ambushed and killed in January 1948.

The Etzion Bloc held out for another two months. Then a convoy which managed to reach it was attacked on its return journey to Jerusalem. There were heavy casualties, and although the survivors were escorted back to Jerusalem by British forces, their arms and vehicles were seized by the attackers.

A day before the declaration of independence on 14 May 1948, a fierce attack was launched on the four settlements. The defenders of Kfar Etzion were killed almost to a man and the others taken prisoner. An Arab refugee camp was set up in Masuot Itzhak, and the Arab Legion took over the strategic high point of Kfar Etzion. But within three months of being captured by the Israel Defence Forces on 7 June 1967, Kfar Etzion was rehabilitated by religious youth including children of the original pioneers.

Some 5 kilometres before reaching Hebron, you see a tall tower, still called by the local inhabitants Burg e-Zur, marking Beit Zur, where Judah the Maccabee fought his most fateful battle. Few architectural remnants are left – only the tower on its square, solid base – but despite its desolation, highlighted by the dozen or two poor Arab dwellings clustered around, the stones of Beit Zur are steeped in memories.

The town stood on the adjoining hillock, Khirbet Tubeika, where signs were found of an early Canaanite settlement and of a large Hyksos town of the middle of the second millennium BC. Destroyed by Egyptian invaders around 1550 BC, it lay in ruins until the coming of the Children of Israel three hundred years later, when 'Halhul, Beth-zur and their villages were allotted to Judah'. Restored by Solomon's son, Rehoboam, who 'built cities for defence in Judah, even Bethlehem and Tekoa and Beth-zur', it flourished after the Return to Zion and under the Greek domination of Palestine from the 4th century BC onward.

With the rising tide of feeling against the Greeks, and the revolt of the Maccabees, Beit Zur increased in importance. The First Book of Maccabees tells how the Greek general

Lysias 'gathered together three score thousand choice men on foot and five thousand horsemen . . . they pitched their tents at Bethsura and Judas met him with ten thousand men'. Judah's troops killed five thousand of Lysias' soldiers and routed his army. Then he and his brothers went up to Jerusalem, cleansed the Temple and immediately afterwards, on 25th of *Kislev*, reconsecrated the altar, declaring an eight-day feast of 'mirth and gladness', the Hanukkah of today.

Beit Zur's vital role was that of a frontier town guarding against enemy incursions from the south, from Edom or Idumea, as it was known in Hasmonean days. Thus when John Hyrcanus defeated and judaized the Edomites in 125 BC, Beit Zur gradually declined. When revived in the Byzantine era, it was refounded on the neighbouring hill, and the tower base is believed to belong to this period. The early Arabs added their part in the 7th century AD; then the Crusaders rebuilt it five hundred years later.

It seems likely that the Byzantines preferred the new site for its proximity to the Spring of St Philip (Ein ed-Dirweh) on the other side of the present main road. Tradition associates the spring with the New Testament story of Acts 8:38, in which Philip baptizes a eunuch. The Madeba map shows Beit Zur with a church, a round pool and an inscription reading 'of Saint Philip. There they say was baptized Candace's eunuch'.

Ein ed-Dirweh is used today to supply the needs of the surrounding villages. A rock clearing makes a convenient meeting-place for the peasant women who come to draw water in their graceful pitchers, while from the clearing a flight of rock-cut steps leads down to the spring.

Genesis 13:18 tells how 'Abram removed his tent, and came and dwelt in the plain of Mamre, which is in Hebron, and built there an altar unto the Lord'. Tradition claims that the site of Abraham's altar is at Ramat el-Khalil, just north of Hebron. Moslem folklore repeatedly refers to Abraham as the Friend of God, or more familiarly as the Friend (*el-Khalil*), and in this way Jaffa Gate, from where Abraham is thought to have left Jerusalem to travel south to Hebron

Mamre

and Beersheba, received its Arabic name of Bab el-Khalil ('Gate of the Friend'). Similarly the site of Abraham's altar is known as Ramat el-Khalil, or sometimes as Beit el-Khalil – ('Height or House of the Friend').

Some 2 kilometres south of Beit Zur and about the same distance north of Hebron, Ramat el-Khalil today consists of a rectangular enclosure roughly 50 by 75 metres in size, encircled by gigantic Herodian ashlars and with a masonry-built well – Bir Avraham ('Well of Abraham') – in the right-hand corner.

Time-honoured tales hold that the Patriarch himself dug this well four thousand years ago, and from it he asked his servants to fetch a little water for his three angelic guests who visited him in Mamre.

Then Abraham bade them, 'wash your feet, and rest yourselves under the tree'. The huge oak or terebinth tree under which they rested was in later years hacked to pieces by souvenir-hungry pilgrims. Its replacement is shown today near the neighbouring Russian monastery.

The compound itself is divided by the well-marked foundations of three parallel cross walls. The middle section holds the traditional stones of Abraham's altar, while to the east are the remains of the Basilica of the Terebinth of Mamre. You can still discern the apse, two side aisles and several small rooms. Greek letters and pilgrim crosses are carved into some of the stones, on one of which is a Greek inscription recording a prayer for someone named Paregorios.

Mamre, with its great tree and adjacent altar, probably became one of the forbidden 'high places' where back-sliding Israelites worshipped pagan gods. It fell with the Babylonian conquest of 586 BC and lost its identity until Herod the Great built the huge enclosure as an open-air temple above Abraham's altar. Later, it served as a khan and market-place, and it was here that the pitiful remnants of Bar-Kokhba's brave army were sold as slaves by the Romans.

After this national calamity, paganism flourished, and Mamre became a centre for heathen practices to such an extent that when Emperor Constantine's mother-in-law visited the Holy Land early in the 4th century AD, she was shocked at what went on at Mamre! At her request, Constantine built the Basilica of the Terebinth there, reconsecrating the ancient sanctuary.

For nearly three centuries, the Basilica of the Terebinth was a favourite pilgrim shrine, but with the Arab conquest of AD 638 it was abandoned. Gradually earth and rubble filled Abraham's well and covered his altar, Herod's proud ramparts fell into decay and Constantine's lovely Byzantine masonry crumbled into heaps of stones. However, as in other places throughout the length and breadth of the Holy Land, the ancient name was not forgotten, and remained the self-same Mamre, or Beit el-Khalil, where 'The Lord appeared unto Abraham in the plains of Mamre: and he sat in the tent door in the heat of the day' (Genesis 18: 1).

Hebron

Hebron is a lively market town of some 50,000 inhabitants who earn a living by agriculture (mainly grape cultivation) and by making pottery, wood carvings and glassware for the flourishing tourist trade. Standing nearly 1,000 metres above sea level, on the ridge road known as the 'Way of the Fathers', or the 'Patriarchs' Way', it has from time immemorial been an important stop-over on this ancient highway lining the northern lands with Shechem, Jerusalem, Beersheba, Hebron and Egypt.

Modern Hebron, some 35 kilometres south of Jerusalem, looks much like any other Arab mountain townlet, with small stone houses melting into the hillside, winding streets and a bustling market-place. Adjoining the market-place is Hebron's one distinctive feature – the traditional tomb of the biblical Patriarchs and their wives, where legends claim that Adam and Eve are also buried. From this tale is said to derive Hebron's other name of Kiryat Arba ('Town of the Four'), as the burial place of the four most famous couples in biblical literature.

Before going into the tomb, glance at the large open cistern just outside. This is the Pool of Hebron where, the Bible tells, David – having executed the murderers of Saul's son, Ishbosheth – 'cut off their hands and their feet, and hanged them up over the pool in Hebron'.

From the water's edge you can see Herod's magnificent rampart around the Tomb of the Patriarchs, as perfect today as it was two thousand years ago. Topped by a pattern of scalloped stones, it is made up of smooth, narrow-bordered ashlars, some measuring up to 8 metres long, and has tall pilasters attached to the thick wall which encloses a rectangle 50 by 30 metres.

Although the Cave of Machpelah was one of Jewry's most revered sites, for centuries Jews were permitted to ascend only to the seventh step of the entrance stairway. From 1948 to 1967 Hebron was completely cut off, but today, after the Six Day War, the Tomb of the

Patriarchs is open to all pilgrims at certain hours of the day.

The impressive staircase, beyond the seventh step, leads up to a Moslem prayer hall. Then a break in the Herodian ramparts takes you into the main mosque, formerly a church erected above the Cave of Machpelah itself. Four square columns mark out a central and two side aisles, while between the columns are the pink-and-white marble cenotaphs, above the graves of Isaac and Rebecca.

Broad reddish flagstones, also Herodian, pave the floor, and a shallow gutter, recalling the time when the court was open to the weather, runs along one margin. Near Isaac's cenotaph is a small marble structure said to cover the opening into the actual cave, which no one but a member of the el-Hamur family (the hereditary guardians of the shrine) is permitted to enter.

Outside the mosque, but within the Herodian rampart, are the cenotaphs of Abraham, Sarah, Jacob and Leah, while yet another, which Moslems accept as the tomb of Joseph, stands in a massively built projection from the ancient wall.

Hebron's history is perhaps longer than that of any other city in the Holy Land, for it was already a thriving Hittite town when Abraham came here around 1,800 BC. It was here that Sarah died, and her wealthy and honoured husband, after suitably polite negotiations, paid Ephron the Hittite a considerable sum (400 shekels of silver) for a burial cave. In this place Sarah was buried, 'in the cave of the field of Machpelah before Mamre: the same is Hebron in the land of Canaan'. In the fullness of time Abraham was laid to rest beside his beloved wife, then Isaac and Rebecca, then Leah and Jacob, who died in Egypt, were buried there.

Hebron maintained its importance, and when the Children of Israel entered the Promised Land, some six centuries after Abraham's day, it was allotted to Caleb of the tribe of Judah. Soon, however, the priestly family of Levi needed extra living space, and they were given Hebron and its suburbs, which became, like Kadesh in Galilee and Shechem in Mount Ephraim, one of the three cities of refuge west of the Jordan. Caleb was left with the 'fields of the city and its villages'.

David, the one-time shepherd boy from Bethlehem, was told by the Lord to go up to Hebron, where he was anointed

The mosque over the Cave of Machpelah

king and reigned over Judah for seven and a half years. Six of his sons were born here, including his favourite, Absalom, the most handsome of all his children. Absalom's mother was Princess Maacah of Gesher, one of the countries across the Jordan, and this combination of royal blood seems to have made the young prince headstrong and ambitious, for he came to Hebron and stirred up rebellion against his father.

When David conquered the Jebusites in about 1000 BC, he moved his capital to Jerusalem and Hebron declined. Only after Solomon's death, when the kingdom was divided, was Hebron rebuilt by Rehoboam, king of Judah;

but this period was short-lived. 'In the fifth year of king Rehoboam, Shishak, king of Egypt ... took the fortified cities pertaining to Judah', records II Chronicles 12:4. (This event is confirmed by the hieroglyphic inscriptions from 925 BC found in the Temple of Karnak, in northern Thebes. Here Shishak listed the cities he had taken, among them Hebron.

Hebron remained in the hands of the Edomites – the enemies from the south – until Judah the Maccabee regained it in 160 BC. More than a hundred years later, Herod the Great made it once more into a pilgrim town by erecting the fine structures still in place above the Tomb of the Patriarchs, building at the same time the enclosure around Abraham's Well and his altar at neighbouring Mamre.

After the fall of Jerusalem in AD 70, Hebron's star waned, although there was a small Jewish community which persisted into Byzantine days. It was the Byzantines who roofed over Herod's open-air compound, turning it into the Church of St Abraham, where (according to Antonius Martyr, who visited Hebron in AD 560) there was a separate section for Jewish worshippers.

Moslems as well as Jews and Christians revere Abraham, so with the Arab invasion of AD 638 the Mosque of Ibrahim replaced St Abraham's Church. It remained a mosque until the coming of the Crusaders and became a mosque again with Saladin's victory in 1187. Saladin kept the building much as it was before, adding only the cenotaphs, a pulpit and a Moslem prayer niche.

Jews, who had been banished from Hebron under the Crusaders, began to drift back; but life was hard, and the numbers settling remained small. A fillip seems to have been given early in the 15th century by the immigration of Italian Jews who brought with them the craft of glass making.

Most authorities believe that glass making, one of the most ancient industries of the Holy Land, began thousands of years ago on the northern coast of Palestine. It flourished around Acre during the Crusader period, and when the Crusaders were driven out in 1291, Venetian knights and their retainers took the art back to their native

Italy. From it developed the world-famous Venetian glass trade, and it may well be that the Italian Jews who re-established glass production in Palestine learnt their craft in studios set up by the home-coming Venetians.

You can spend a fascinating hour in one of Hebron's small, one-family glass factories watching jewel-coloured blobs of glass being melted in a furnace, then quickly blown into a dish, jug or vase. Working at a remarkably high speed, the glass-blower can turn out dozens of attractive items in a few hours, filling his drab surroundings with beauty. Incidentally, Hebron glass bowls and vases make wonderful and inexpensive gifts.

From the Moslem period onwards, great progress took place in Hebron. Conditions remained static, the chief occupations, then as now, being grape growing and making souvenirs for pilgrims and visitors. Never particularly good, relations between Hebron's Jews and Arabs worsened under the British Mandate, culminating in the 1929 massacre of peaceful Jewish citizens and theological students. Their bodies lie in a common grave in Hebron's hilltop cemetery. Despite this tragic incident, some Jews stayed on in the town until the rioting of 1936, when they were forced to leave, returning only after the Six Day War. Minimal damage was done to lives and property, and for the first time in Hebron's long history the Cave of Machpelah was not occupied by the victors.

Jewish civilians were not encouraged to settle in Hebron, but despite official disapproval, a group of militant orthodox young people defied the military ban and moved there. For several years they lived within the police compound, but today they are housed in blocks of modern apartments and have their own schools, shops and other facilities. Most of the inhabitants of Kiryat Arba (as the settlement is now called) have employment in Jerusalem, but some light industry is being started on the spot. There is no doubt that these determined, energetic settlers have established what will be a politically influential unit on the outskirts of the 'City of the Patriarchs'.

Eshtemoa and Susiya

Biblical Eshtemoa is located 14 kilometres south of Hebron.
First mentioned in the book of Joshua as part of the inheritance
of Judah, it is afterwards stated that 'To the sons of Aaron they
gave the cities of Judah, namely Hebron the city of refuge,
Libnah ... and Jattir, and Eshtemoa, with their suburbs'.
Another biblical reference to the town came in David's time,
when he sent part of the spoil of his victory over the Amale-
kites at Ziklag 'unto the elders of Judah which were in Bethel ... to them which were in Jattir and to them which were
in Eshtemoa'.

Eusebius of Caesarea, the 3rd-century AD geographer,
marked it in his classic gazetteer (the *Onomasticon*) as a
'populous Jewish village'. Archaeological evidence does
indeed prove the existence of a Byzantine townlet. Then
written sources are silent on Eshtemoa until the Crusaders
built a fortress there abutting on the synagogue's western
wall.

An Arab village, es-Samua, echoing the name of three
thousand years ago, stands on the site of Joshua's city. Straight
away you notice a difference between this and other villages,
for here you find house after house with beautifully carved
stones – some with grapes, some with leaves, one with a
menora – incorporated into the stonework.

At the highest point in es-Samua are the partially restored remains
of a late 4th-century AD synagogue of the unusual broadhouse type,
with its entrance on the east. Four massive pillars edge the mosaic-
paved, narrow forecourt with its much-damaged inscriptions, and
this leads on to a doorway into a hall measuring about 15 by 22 metres.
Opposite the entry the west wall, reinforced by Crusader construction, stands to a height of nearly 9 metres, while in the middle of
the broad north wall, facing towards Jerusalem, is a place for the Ark.
Two-tiered stone benches line the north and south sides, and patches
of white mosaics show where the floor had been roughly repaired.
A Moslem praying alcove (a late addition) is set towards the south.
The Torah shrine takes the form of a 4.30-metre-wide projection
into the hall, which hides the original shrine consisting of a central

niche with smaller ones on either side, the whole extending outwards.

Es-Samua was identified with Eshtemoa of the Bible as early as 1830, but the synagogue – the first to be found south of Jerusalem – was discovered and excavated only in 1934. Arab riots two years later prevented the completion of the dig, which was not resumed until 1969, after the Six Day War. Among other finds was the Aramaic inscription in the forecourt, blessing Eleazer the priest and his sons, who donated a sum of 'tirmizim' (a Roman coin) to the synagogue.

Most extraordinary was the find made by the Arab foreman, who brought to light five earthenware jars from the Israelite period (9th and 8th centuries BC). These jars were filled with silver jewellery, ingots and small silver objects, the total cache weighing 25 kilograms – the largest silver hoard ever found in Israel. This treasure trove arouses much speculation. It might have been a single individual's life savings or the stock-in-trade of a silversmith three thousand years ago. It might be – by a long stretch of the imagination – a part of David's plunder from Ziklag given to the elders of Eshtemoa!

The synagogue at Khirbet Susiya, also of the rare broadhouse type, was more elaborate and seems to have had a longer active life than that at Eshtemoa, barely 3 kilometres away. Although already mentioned in 1937 by the investigators of the Eshtemoa synagogue, work at Susiya was begun only in January 1971.

A fabulous mosaic with two menoras in brilliant hues flanking a Torah shrine was revealed early on in the dig. So cleverly handled are the red and orange candle flames that they seem to twinkle as you look at them! Beneath the menoras are the Jewish symbols of the ram's horn and palm frond (lulav), while a wistful-eyed horse gazes up at the flickering lights.

As clearing continued, the plan of the compound became distinct. A forecourt some 16 metres broad by 12 metres deep had two entrance gateways – one on the east and one on the north – and grand pillared arcades along the north, east and south sides. To the west – the longer side – a flight of stairs ascended to the narrow vestibule in front of the prayer hall. Inside the hall you see two carpet-like mosaic pavements, while tiers of stone benches rise on the left (south) wall, on the west

A mosaic inscription discovered at Susiya

and on part of the north. Solidly built throughout, some of the walls are two metres thick, and none are less than one metre.

Of particular interest are the synagogue inscriptions, recently published by the archaeological team working there. Some were chiselled into the pillars and some into the stone balustrades, while four were set into the mosaic floors. Two of these, written in Aramaic, were found in the vestibule, and seem to be the familiar acknowledgement of gifts offered to the synagogue. The third – one of the very few of this date in Hebrew – is unique in the fact that it reckons the placing of the tablet from the year of the Creation. This tablet was on the threshold just inside the hall.

Complete and undamaged was another Hebrew inscription, this time from the southern arcade of the forecourt, praising various benefactors of the synagogue. One is specially thanked for plastering the synagogue walls and providing the material to do so!

According to the archaeological findings, the synagogue at Khirbet Susiya was established at the end of the 4th century or the beginning of the 5th century AD and served a large and wealthy community. It underwent many repairs, changes and restorations and continued to be a centre of Jewish life well into the 9th, possibly even the 10th century AD, when for some reason the district was abandoned and the buildings disintegrated.

The Road to Ramalla

Travelling north from Jerusalem on the timeless 'Way of the Fathers', you have the feeling that little has changed here for two millennia and more. The ancient caravan route from Mesopotamia to Egypt ran along the central range – the hills of Judea and Samaria – acting both as a highway and as the division between the fertile western valleys, like Dotan and Ayalon, and the arid scrub-land to the east.

On your journey you see the carefully terraced hills, tended by Arabs as they were in Israelite times to prevent the soil being washed away by the rain. You see the green valleys ploughed and sown and flocks of sheep and goats seeking sustenance, as they did in the days of the Patriarchs, in the dry, semi-desert rolling down to the Jordan Valley and the Dead Sea.

Although most of the road is through agricultural land, here and there are urban settlements, some very luxurious, like Shuafat, a residential suburb some 5 kilometres north of the capital. Wealthy Arab families and foreign diplomats live in these lovely homes, gleaming with polished stone and decorated with graceful iron grilles, above which rises Tel el-Ful ('Hill of the Bean'). On its summit sprawls an unfinished, rambling structure which, before the Six Day War, was intended to be the summer residence of King Hussein of Jordan.

The outcome of the Six Day War, however, changed these plans, and Tel el-Ful, said to take its name from the crops of beans and peas that thrived on its chalky soil, became once more the biblical Gibeah of the tribe of Benjamin. Here King Saul lived three thousand years ago, and here was the dramatic setting of the Bible tale of the Levite from Mount Ephraim, who 'took a concubine out of Bethlehem-judah'. Unhappy in her new life, she ran back to her father's house, and when her husband came to fetch her, they decided not to stay overnight in Jerusalem, then still in Canaanite hands, for, said the Levite, 'We will not turn into the city of a stranger, we will pass over into Gibeah.' Here the woman was attacked by 'certain sons of Belial . . . who abused her all night until the morning', when she was found dying.

The Benjaminites refused to bring the culprits to justice, so the Levite cut up the body and sent a piece to each of the Twelve Tribes, demanding their help to avenge the murder. This incident sparked off a civil war, which ended only when Gibeah of the time of the Judges was razed, and 'the flames began to rise out of the city with a pillar of smoke'.

Down the years, Gibeah's disgrace was forgiven to the extent that Israel's first king was chosen from the tribe of Benjamin. The son of Kish, a man of Benjamin who is believed to have lived in nearby Beit Hanina, Saul was 'a choice young man and goodly . . . from his shoulders and upward he was higher than any of the people'. After being anointed by the prophet Samuel, Saul chose the dominating height of Gibeah to build his unpretentious palace. Twenty years later this, too, was destroyed by fire, then under David's united rule it fell into disuse. When the kingdom was split up, Gibeah, or

Gleaning wheat in the rich fields of Samaria

Givat Shaul ('Height of Saul') as it was often called, became a frontier post.

All these phases in the history of Tel el-Ful are reflected in its archaeological finds. Among the earliest excavations to be carried out in Palestine, it was dug in 1922 and 1923, then in 1933 by Professor W. F. Albright, who brought to light several strata, the lowest being that of Gibeah of the Judges, showing clear signs of destruction by fire. Above it was Saul's citadel-palace – a large, two-storied structure with four corner towers, well-equipped by the standards of those days. Storage jars for wine, oil and wheat; painted and burnished bowls, plates and juglets; spindle whorls and agricultural tools revealed the comparatively comfortable life of the palace. A layer of ashes was a silent witness that this was burnt, possibly by the encroaching Philistines.

Remains from the 9th and 8th centuries BC showed a fort with a tower and sloping defence wall made of stones from the earlier building. Crude earthenware jars and cooling pots stressed that here was a purely military outpost, with no frills or refinements! Since then, Tel el-Ful, the biblical Gibeah, has been no more than a village or an isolated strongpoint, but never again did it attain the dignity of a royal capital as it was three thousand years ago.

The little-known settlement of Neve Ya'akov, about 2 kilometres north of the suburb of Shuafat, was founded in 1924 and named for the religious Zionist leader Rabbi Ya'akov Reiness. Its members raised cattle, were dairy farmers and also worked at afforestation, forming an industrious, productive Jewish island in an Arab sea. For twenty-four years they carried on steadily with their daily tasks, but the growing tension preceding the 1948 War of Independence made their position untenable, and in May 1948 they were forced to withdraw. The Arab Legion promptly set up a camp there.

Following the Six Day War, work immediately began on a huge housing estate there comprising thousands of living units, roads, schools and shops – a living memorial to the heroes of Neve Ya'akov who held the land for twenty-four long and dangerous years.

The prophet Samuel, like many other giants of the biblical world, is held in high esteem by Moslems as well as Jews. His traditional grave at Nebi Samwil (literally the 'Prophet Samuel'), today marked by a mosque and towering minaret, can be reached by travelling for 10 kilometres or so on a side road branching left (west) from Beit Hanina. Its commanding position has made Nebi Samwil a vital strategic point between Jerusalem and the coast, and even in the present century it has changed hands several times.

Here, in 1917, the British gained a decisive victory over the Turks; here the Arab Legion was entrenched during the 1948 War of Independence, and in June 1967, the Israel Defence Forces attacked and conquered the height, making possible the opening up of the Old City.

Graceful pointed arches and buttressed walls incorporated into the mosque indicate Crusader origins, and it is generally accepted that the building was part of a Crusader church. A huge cenotaph stands in the central aisle above Samuel's grave, while behind the cenotaph is a shute, possibly used to slide bodies into the crypt. On either side are oblong stone slabs said to be the graves of Samuel's parents, El-kanah and Hanna, and in the crypt, almost filled by an enormous sarcophagus, niches for lamps or candles are hollowed out of the walls to hold propitiary lights – a widespread custom among Jews and Christians.

Nebi Samwil, the focal point of a tiny, run-down Arab hamlet, is thought to be biblical Ramah, where Samuel was born, where he had his own home and where he was buried. Here it was that 'the elders of Israel . . . came to Samuel unto Ramah' and here he died, and 'the Israelites gathered together, and lamented him, and buried him in his house in Ramah'.

The belief that this was indeed Samuel's tomb persisted down the ages, and a commemorative basilica was erected here by the 6th-century Byzantine emperor Justinian. Always a pilgrim centre, Jews made a special point of pilgrimage on the 28th of the Hebrew month of *Iyar*, the anniversary of Samuel's death, while at the beginning of the 11th century, a Karaite synagogue is thought to have stood somewhere nearby. A hundred years later, the Crusaders built their church on the same hill, which they called Montjoy – a happy name given to it by Christians journeying through Palestine in the Middle Ages, for from here they caught their first glimpse of the walls of Jerusalem. Richard the Lionhearted, however, coming after the Moslem capture of the city, found the hill far from joyful, and stories tell how he stood and wept as he looked towards the Holy City which he could not enter.

Few changes have taken place in this sleepy part of the countryside, but a brave attempt at Jewish settlement was made in 1888, when Rabbi Isaac Rivlin bought 500 acres of farmland there and apportioned it out to thirteen Yemenite families. The project was unsuccessful, despite hard work and willingness to live in this overwhelmingly Arab-populated area, and within three years it was broken up. At the moment another effort is being made to encourage Jewish residents to come here, and multi-storied apartment houses are quickly rising at neighbouring Ramot.

The quiet hill village of Qubeibe, about 4 kilometres beyond Nebi Samwil, has for centuries been a storm-centre of theological discussion. Was Qubeibe – La Petite Mahomerie ('The Little Dome' or 'Little Mosque' of the Crusaders) – the Emmaus of the New Testament, or does Amwas, near Latrun, have the distinction of being the spot where Jesus met Cleophas and Simon after his resurrection?

Based largely on what could be considered a reasonable day's journey for those times of getting from place to place on foot or at best on donkey-back, Qubeibe seems to fit in with the disciples' programme. After Jesus had been buried, these two disciples 'went that same day to a village called Emmaus', and following the miraculous events that had occurred that evening 'they rose up the same hour and returned to Jerusalem.

Luke's story tells how Cleophas and his companion, having arrived home at twilight, met a stranger and asked him to 'Abide with us; for it is toward evening and the day is far spent'. This was the risen Jesus, who accepted their invitation, but quickly vanished. Realizing what had happened, the two men hurried back to Jerusalem to spread the news.

No more than a tenuous tradition linked Qubeibe with Emmaus, and it would have remained so had it not been for a remarkable woman – the Marchioness Pauline Nicolay. Born in Paris in 1811, she was a devout Catholic who came here on a pilgrimage and was told of this legend. Convinced of its truth, Pauline came to live in Qubeibe and in 1861 bought a plot of land there on which stood, in her own words, 'an ancient room', eventually found to be the chapel of the Crusader settlement. Offering this land to the Franciscan Order, she was met with disbelief and even resentment, but in 1867, when Pauline had left Qubeibe and joined the Casa Nova Convent in Jerusalem, her gift was accepted. Afterwards, investigators discovered the remains of a Crusader basilica built over the remnants of the traditional House of Cleophas.

Later excavations adjacent to the church revealed a whole Crusader village with houses on either side of what was the main Roman, then the Crusader, road from the coast through Latrun, Qubeibe and Nebi Samwil to Jerusalem. These one-room dwellings, some quite large, have courtyards and primitive ovens, while there seems also to have been a communal bakery and wine press. Beneath the Crusader structures were found Byzantine and Roman remains.

When you visit the village of Qubeibe, look out for the big walled convent, originally built in 1912 as a leprosarium, and note the welcoming 'Mane Nobiscum Dominus' ('Abide with us, Master') over the gates of the Franciscan church and monastery. Inside the church, erected in 1901, watch particularly for the sections of Crusader masonry standing several metres high, the glass-covered foundation of the House of Cleophas and, in the left-hand aisle, the tomb of the Marchioness Pauline Nicolay, that extraordinary woman who did not live to see the vindication of her unwavering faith.

El-Jib, a picturesque Arab village about 6 kilometres west of Beit Hanina, adjoins the site of biblical Gibeon. Today a small agricultural settlement of simple, hard-working farmers, the Gibeon of 3,500 years ago was 'a great city, one of the royal cities' – the only Canaanite city-state to come to terms with

The pool at Gibeon

the invading Israelites. Because of this treaty, it was attacked by an alliance of other Canaanite kingdoms, and was defended by Joshua, who pleaded with the Lord to make the 'Sun stand still upon Gibeon'. God granted his prayer, and the sun lighted up the battlefield until victory was won.

What makes el-Jib different from any other village in the vicinity is its great rock-cut pool, which measures more than 12 metres across and about the same in depth, with a spiral stairway descending to the bottom. An unusual feature of the stairway is the edging of mother rock forming a protective balustrade.

The stairs reach a sealed stone trap-door and continue beyond it for another 15 metres below the ground level of the pool into a spring-fed water-chamber, accessible also by walking round the outside of the pool. This and other springs, which once filled the elaborate cistern still provide the main water supply for the villagers.

This strange reservoir, dug soon after Joshua's conquest of the Promised Land, was discovered during Professor J. B. Pritchard's excavations of 1956-9. His team, sponsored by Princeton University, also found curious underground wine stores from the time of the First Temple. These can be seen close to the upper level of the pool, where there are many rock-hewn wine presses and a broad stretch of white rock with no less than sixty-three smooth round openings branching into flask-like hollows, each about $2\frac{1}{2}$ metres deep. Professor Pritchard also unearthed Canaanite tombs from 2000 to 1200 BC, as well as Roman burials of the turn of the Christian era.

Bible stories come alive when you see the very place where David's followers met those of his rival to the throne – Saul's son Ishbosheth – 'at the pool of Gibeon'. The groups faced each other across the pool and in the ensuing fight Ishbosheth's men were defeated. During most of David's reign and the beginning of Solomon's, the Tabernacle was housed at Gibeon while the Temple was being completed, and the Bible tells how Solomon 'went to Gibeon to sacrifice there'. He offered up a thousand burnt offerings, and asked the Lord for 'an understanding heart to judge thy people'.

Evidence of the wealth and fruitfulness of Gibeon during the First Temple period was found in the sixty-three wine cellars, which were filled by 36-litre earthenware jars kept cool by the natural rock. Up to 100,000 litres could be stored at any one time, and stamped jar handles, inscribed in ancient Hebrew, bore the words 'Gibeon: vineyard of Amariah' (or Azariah, or Hananiah, as the case might be).

Destroyed during the Babylonian invasion of 586 BC, Gibeon recovered with the Return to Zion and developed into a prosperous town, continuing to be so during Roman times and after. It became a peaceful, thriving farming community, ready to compromise as it had done with Joshua in 1250 BC, so it remained on an even keel in the midst of the turbulent events going on all around.

Atarot, Jerusalem's airport, just over 10 kilometres north of the capital, was formerly known as Kalandia, from the name of the Arab village nearby. Established under the British Mandate mainly for its army and VIP traffic, it quickly became an important factor in the military set-up of the contemporary governing power.

Jewish settlement in the area began in 1912, well before the airport was started, when the Jewish National Fund bought agricultural land adjoining Kalandia. In 1914 came a group of young pioneers, including nineteen-year-old Russian immigrant Levi Shkolnik (later Levi Eshkol, Israel's Prime Minister from 1963 until his death in 1969), who made their homes there under extremely difficult conditions. These dauntless youngsters built the simplest of houses for themselves, worked the fields and used water from the local spring for their day-to-day needs. They called the place Atarot, after an ancient town said to have existed in the region.

This first experiment was cut short by the outbreak of World War One, but a successful *moshav* (cooperative village) was set up in 1922 and flourished until obliged to leave its land in 1948 (but not before fourteen Jews were killed in an Arab ambush). The settlers moved to the abandoned German colony of Wilhelmina, on the outskirts of Lydda, which was renamed Bnei Atarot ('Children of Atarot').

Ramalla and Environs

A pleasant holiday town about 15 kilometres north of Jerusalem, Ramalla stands on a hill ridge nearly 900 metres above sea level. Together with its twin-town, Bireh, it has some 26,000 inhabitants and is a favourite summer resort for residents of Judea and Samaria, being cool and breezy even on the hottest day.

Ramalla's outstanding landmark is the soaring antenna attached to the relay station on the highest point of the hill. Established during the British Mandate, it was the base for Jewish broadcasting until 1948, when it was taken over by the Jordanians and used for the same purpose until the Six Day War, when Ramalla was captured and the station immediately absorbed into Israel's radio and television network.

Bireh, Ramalla's Moslem twin-town and ancient counterpart, is famed for its rich springs and rose gardens. Identified with biblical Beeroth, it is also known in Christian tradition as the place where, on the journey back from the Passover pilgrimage to Jerusalem, Mary and Joseph noticed that the boy Jesus was missing. They returned to the capital, and 'found him in the Temple, sitting in the midst of the doctors, both hearing them and asking them questions'.

In Crusader times it was an administrative district called La Grande Mahomerie ('The Large Dome'), in contradistinction to neighbouring Qubeibe, known as La Petite Mahomerie. Settled by farming families from among the Crusaders themselves, Bireh was destroyed by Saladin in 1187 and its fields and homesteads taken over by Moslem peasants, whose descendants may well be living there until today.

Little is left of biblical Shiloh where, in the days of Joshua, 'the Children of Israel assembled together and set up the tabernacle of the congregation'. Now known as Khirbet Seilun ('ruins of Shiloh'), the place where the Ark of the Lord was housed for two hundred years is now nothing but heaps of stones steeped in a brooding sense of history.

Khirbet Seilun, about 20 kilometres north of Ramalla, is

The ruins of Shiloh

close to the one-time Crusader hamlet of Sinjil (a corruption of the family name of St Gilles) and even closer to the Arab village of Turmous Aiye, once a thriving Roman town. Incidentally, the finely carved 2nd-century AD sarcophagus shown in the Citadel of Jerusalem was unearthed here.

Skirting Turmous Aiye, you approach ancient Shiloh and first notice the remains of Jamia es-Sittin ('Mosque of the Sixty'), where sixty Crusader knights were cut down by the Moslems. Here, above the traditional graves of Eli the priest and of his sons, Hophni and Phineas, was a 2nd- or 3rd-century AD synagogue. Until a little while ago a huge stone lintel, decorated with an amphora and olive wreaths and possibly belonging to this early synagogue, could be seen on the spot.

One day it disappeared, to be found buried in a field and transferred to the Rockefeller Museum.

Before reaching the *tel* itself, you see the foundations of two Byzantine churches with pillars, bases and capitals strewn around and with mosaic floors now covered for protection. Beyond is a strange little structure (Jamia el-Ittim) made up of massive stones from Roman or even earlier times. An enormous worked stone forms the lintel, and steps on the side lead up to the roof, which is shaded by a spreading terebinth tree.

Jamia el-Ittim is on the edge of the extensive excavations made by the Danish expedition of 1926, which shed much light on Shiloh's past. Houses and household utensils from the time of the Judges – the period when Shiloh was the home of the Holy Ark – were found, and this layer shows signs of having been burnt, perhaps when the Philistines carried off the Ark.

Tracing Shiloh's history with the help of the Bible and the archaeologist's spade, a picture is drawn of a village of the time of Abraham, undocumented except for scraps of pottery dug up on the site. Upon it, around 1250 BC, a camp was struck by Joshua and his followers, and here the Tabernacle was set up, and 'the Children of Israel divided for an inheritance by lot in Shiloh'. For two centuries and more, Shiloh remained the heart of the infant nation, and here it was that Elkanah and Hanna, his barren wife, went up 'to worship and to sacrifice unto the Lord of hosts in Shiloh'. Their faith was rewarded, and Hanna bore a son, Samuel, whom she 'brought unto the house of the Lord in Shiloh'.

Later came the battle with the Philistines, the capture of the Ark and the loss of Shiloh's prestige. However, with the Return to Zion, Shiloh began to revive, and there was a small but continuous settlement through the Hasmonean, Herodian and Roman eras, while the basilicas show it was a Byzantine pilgrim centre. On the 6th-century AD Madeba map it appears with the remark 'Shiloh there once the Ark!' It was suddenly abandoned around 1300 AD, and since then nothing was built and nothing grows in Shiloh, the first home of the Tabernacle, where 'the child Samuel grew before the Lord' (I Samuel 2:21).

Nablus and Environs

About 22 kilometres northwards from the entrance to Shiloh you reach Mount Gerizim and Mount Ebal, which stand like sentinels on either side of Nablus and of ancient Shechem. At their closest point the two are barely 100 metres apart, with Mount Gerizim lying to the south and Mount Ebal to the north. Gerizim is 880 metres above sea level, while bleak Mount Ebal reaches 940 metres.

These two hills appear very early in biblical literature. Even before the Children of Israel crossed the Jordan River they were told by Moses to 'set up great stones and plaster them with plaster, and write upon them all the words of this law ... and set them up in Mount Ebal'. Moses also commanded that six of the tribes – Simeon, Levi, Judah, Issachar, Joseph and Benjamin – should stand on Mount Gerizim to bless the people, and the other six – Reuben, Gad, Asher, Zebulun, Dan and Naphtali – should curse them from Mount Ebal.

Shortly after crossing into the Promised Land, Joshua fulfilled Moses' commandment and 'built an altar unto the Lord God of Israel in mount Ebal ... and wrote upon the stones a copy of the law of Moses'. An interesting sidelight on the Samaritan version of the Torah shows that in their transcription of Deuteronomy 27:12 (Moses' injunction to set up the stones of the Law on Mount Ebal), Ebal is replaced by Mount Gerizim!

Mount Gerizim, the holy mountain of the Samaritans, to which they turn during prayer, is the scene of three annual pilgrimages according to Mosaic Law, those of Passover, Pentecost and Tabernacles. Particularly impressive is the Samaritan Passover when, as in olden days, the white-clad priests sacrifice a lamb, and the feast is celebrated in a lively fashion.

On the hilltop a mosque marks the traditional grave of Sheikh Ghanem, a native of Samaria and friend of Saladin. Adjoining it are the foundations of an octagonal structure – a church dating from about 485 AD built by Roman emperor Zeno. Destroyed during the Samaritan riots against the

Christians, it was rebuilt by Justinian, and you can still see the encircling walls with corner towers which he put up.

The Samaritans are a people whose origins derived from the 9th century BC, when Samaria was a prosperous city set in fertile surroundings. But as often happens when material comforts grow too great, many of its people turned to pagan worship. Unheeded warnings were given by the Prophet Elijah, by Elisha and by Amos the herdsman, and in 722 BC Samaria was overrun by the Assyrians. Thirty thousand of Samaria's citizens were sold into slavery, and outsiders were brought in to repopulate and work the decimated countryside. They intermarried with and took on the religion of the local inhabitants, accepting only the Pentateuch and not the rest of the Bible. They called themselves Samaritans, and claimed theirs to be the true Mosaic faith. Two groups still exist in the Holy Land – a small one in Holon, near Tel Aviv and a larger one in this very area.

When the exiles returned from Babylon they found a people that were strange to them, for generations of absorbing different cultures had left indelible impressions on both sides. The rift was widened when representatives came to Zerubabel, a Judean nobleman, who refused their offered help in rebuilding the Temple. Hurt and offended, the local spokesman said 'we seek your God, as ye do; and we do sacrifice unto him since the days of Esar-haddon', and in defiance the Samaritans set up a centre in Shechem and built a rival temple on Mount Gerizim.

The books of Ezra and Nehemiah tell of the break between the Jewish exiles returning from Babylon and those who had remained in the land. Josephus further tells how Manasseh the priest, barred from his office for marrying a local woman, was promised by his father-in-law, Sanballat, a priesthood and 'a temple like that at Jerusalem, upon Mount Gerizim'.

To find the vanished temple of the Samaritans has always been an archaeologist's dream, and in recent years this has come close to fulfilment. Excavations on Tel e-Ras, on the eastern slope of Gerizim, had previously revealed a temple to Zeus with monumental stairways, erected by Emperor Hadrian. In 1968 a team sponsored by the American School of Oriental Research in Jerusalem dug below it and found

Jacob's Well

an imposing building from the time of Alexander the Great which had been partially destroyed by burning. It is now believed that this was the original Samaritan temple, built in the 4th century BC and razed by Hasmonean John Hyrcanus in 128 BC.

At the foot of Mount Ebal, in the village of Askar (ancient Sychar), is the Well of Jacob. Although not explicitly mentioned in the Old Testament, Jacob's Well appears in the New Testament tale of how Jesus left Judea and went to Galilee. On his journey he came to a 'city of Samaria, called Sychar, near the parcel of ground Jacob gave to his son Joseph. Now Jacob's well was there.'

The traditional site of the well was already firmly established in 333 AD, when the Bordeaux Pilgrim wrote his chronicle. First referred to as a sacred pool used as a baptistry, it had a cross-shaped church built over it by the early Byzantines (it was destroyed during the Samaritan risings and rebuilt by Emperor Justinian in the 6th century AD. In 1130, the Crusaders erected a new basilica above the well, but with the end of the Crusader régime it fell into decay. The site itself remained a place of pilgrimage, and it was bought by the Greek-Orthodox Patriarchate in 1860, when an agreement was entered into with the Russian-Orthodox Church to put up a magnificent building upon the ruins. With the Russian upheaval in World War One, their support was withdrawn, and today the unfinished monument stands in a walled garden, awaiting the day of its completion.

Tel Balata, on which stand the impressive ruins of biblical Shechem, is but a few minutes away from Jacob's Well. The town of Shechem is referred to again and again in Bible stories, for it was an important station on the 'Patriarchs' Way' and already a city of importance when Abraham made his way south from Haran to Sichem in the land of Canaan, and there 'builded he an altar unto the Lord'.

For sixty years or more the site has been an archaeologists' paradise. A German team began to work there in 1913 and continued at intervals until 1934, while another group under George Ernest Wright of Harvard University made five major excavations of ancient Shechem between 1956 and 1964.

What can be seen today is the solid city wall of Hyksos times (18th–16th centuries BC) with its sloping glacis and massive masonry; the open-air temple showing curious upright pillars; and the gigantic eastern gate with a broad staircase leading down into the town. This distinctive double gate was first built at the end of the Hyksos era, then destroyed and reconstructed several times.

Archaeological findings revealed that there was a Chalcolithic community here two thousand years before Abraham appeared and that during his time and in the centuries that followed Shechem was without doubt one of the largest and most important cities in the land of Canaan. When Jacob came to Shechem, he found it settled by Hivites (a Canaanite race) who were governed by Hamor and his son, Shechem. From them Jacob bought a piece of land and set up an altar, but the Hebrews' good relations with the Hivites were shattered by the sad tale of rape, murder and broken promises told in Genesis 34.

It was in Shechem that Joshua assembled the Children of Israel in order that they might take upon themselves the privileges and the obligations of the Holy Law, and it was there that the bones of Joseph, who had died in Egypt, were brought by the Children of Israel and 'buried in Shechem in a parcel of ground which Jacob bought of the sons of Hamor . . . for a hundred pieces of silver'.

An influential town at the time of the Judges, Shechem was the background of the struggle for power after Gideon's death. One of his unofficial wives was a woman of Shechem, who bore Gideon a son, Abimelech. Abimelech conspired with his mother's kin, killed his seventy brothers (all but Jotham, the youngest) and they 'made Abimelech king, by the plains of the pillar that was in Shechem'.

Shechem seems to have kept up its royal reputation, for 'Rehoboam went to Shechem; for all Israel were come to Shechem to make him king'. Here it was that the revolt broke out and the kingdom split into two, with Jeroboam of Israel setting up his first capital there.

Ruins of ancient Shechem

When the kings of Israel moved their capital to Samaria, Shechem declined. It declined still further after the Assyrian conquest of Israel in 722 BC, and eventually, in 128 BC, it was abandoned. In its stead, in AD 72 Titus founded Nablus (Neopolis, or 'New Town') upon the site of the adjacent Jewish village of Maabarta and named it Flavia Neopolis in honour of his father, Flavius Vespasian.

In its early days, strategic Nablus, which protected the pass from the Mediterranean through the hills to the Jordan Valley, was mainly a Samaritan centre and a settlement town

Nablus

for veteran Roman soldiers, who were afforded special privileges if they made their permanent homes in certain areas.
With the rise of Christianity, Nablus developed as a Christian
town, with fine churches and other institutions, but AD 529
saw a revolt of the Samaritans, who murdered the bishop and
all the monks and sacked the monasteries and churches.
Emperor Justinian put down the rebellion with a heavy hand,
killing many of the rebels and selling 20,000 as slaves. Only
a sprinkling of Samaritans were left in the formerly Samaritan
town of Nablus.

A Samaritan Passover celebration

Occupied by the Arabs in AD 636, it was a rich and comfortable city when taken without a fight by the Crusaders. Nablus thrived under their rule, too, and Queen Melissande of Jerusalem, whose particular domain it was, encouraged building and development.

Modern Nablus is the chief city of the district of Samaria with a population of some 45,000, practically all Moslem Arabs with a sprinkling of Christians and Samaritans. Now, as in the past, it has a flourishing soap and olive-oil industry based on the olive orchards that clothe the surrounding hills, and the soap of Nablus is famed throughout the countries of the Middle East.

Nablus is also the trading centre for the villages in the whole vicinity, and its lively markets are packed with local produce, particularly with the agricultural products brought in by the farmers. Apart from the markets and soap factories, there is little in Nablus itself to interest the tourist, for of the many beautiful structures erected in Byzantine and Crusader times, much was destroyed in the severe earthquake of 1927, much was built over and much simply taken to pieces and the stones reused. Practically the only place where you can see earlier building is in the Great Mosque (Jamia el-Kabir), where there are Crusader and Byzantine remains.

The earthquake of 1927 also damaged the old Samaritan synagogue beyond repair, and it has now been rebuilt and houses the Samaritan's greatest treasure – the oldest extant Samaritan Scroll of the Law.

A Samaritan with the Scrolls of the Law

Samaria

Samaria, about 8 kilometres north-west of Shechem, is perhaps the most spectacular of the historical sites of the Holy

Double-scrolled capitals at Sebaste

Land. Once the rich capital of the kings of Israel, later Herod's grand city of Sebaste and afterwards a thriving Roman town, enough of it remains to draw a vivid picture of the might and majesty of Samaria in its heyday.

Today the drab village of Sebastiye, its Moslem Arab inhabitants mostly occupied as caretakers for the site and its visiting tourists, adjoins the former capital. Passing through the village, look out for the mosque, originally the Crusader Cathedral of St John the Baptist, where his head is reputedly buried. Beneath the courtyard you will be shown a crypt with the traditional graves of the prophets Elisha and Obadiah.

Walking around the partially restored ruins of Samaria, you will be able to identify several periods. Rows of pillars mark the Roman forum, which has a Byzantine basilica at one end of it and the wall of King Ahab's 9th-century BC palace on the other. Beyond is the Greek round tower of the 4th century BC, the Herodian theatre and temple and an early Church of St John, with granite columns and massive ashlars, while on the crest of the hill are the foundations of the citadel of Samaria. Encircling the hill is a colonnaded street with solid city gates, guard towers and bays for shops and for people to gather.

The first question that springs to your mind is probably 'Who were the kings of Israel?' Their origin dates back to 933 BC, when Solomon died and his kingdom was inherited by his headstrong son, Rehoboam. Rehoboam tried to increase his revenues by increasing the already high taxes and came into conflict with his subjects because 'he forsook the counsel of the old men . . . and consulted with the young men that were grown up with him'. As a result, the land was divided into the Kingdom of Judah to the south and the Kingdom of Israel to the north. Judah, comprising the tribes of Judah and Benjamin, had Rehoboam as its king and Jerusalem as its capital, while Israel was ruled by Jeroboam, one of Solomon's most able officers.

Whatever their faults, the kings of Israel were good and capable planners. Their earlier capital, nearby Tirza, was well laid out and built on a high standard. Then, when the army man, Omri, seized power in 887 BC, 'he bought the hill of Samaria of Shemer for two talents of silver', and then

Sebaste

proceeded to build a new city on the untouched mountain.

Some of Omri's hilltop enclave still stands, and archaeologists have revealed the luxurious fashion in which it was constructed. Ahab, Omri's son, extended the palace, adding an extra protective rampart, stabling for hundreds of chariots and horses and the 'ivory house' referred to in I Kings 22:39. Among the finds were a number of massive columns with the typical First Temple period double-scrolled capitals like those discovered in Megiddo, Hazor and Ramat Rachel, while even more remarkable were the delicately carved ivory panels and figurines, some embellished with gold and yet others inscribed with Hebrew-Phoenician characters.

Ahab's domestic policy was shadowed by the bad influence of his wife, Jezebel, whose name is a symbol of evil until today. On the international scene, however, he was an outstanding figure, and among the records of Shalmaneser III of Assyria is one telling how he fought a coalition of three kings – 'Hadadezer of Damascus, with 1,200 chariots; Irhuleni of Hamath with 700 chariots; and Ahab the Israelite, with 2,000 chariots.'

Around 330 BC Alexander of Macedon conquered Samaria, rebuilding it as a Grecian and pagan city, thus angering the remnant of conforming Jews. Papyrus scrolls from that time, recently found near Jerusalem in a cave filled with human bones, shed new light on this little-known era. The scrolls tell how Hananiah ben-Sanballat, governor of Samaria, possibly the great-grandson of the Sanballat of the book of Nehemiah, took part in an unsuccessful rising against Alexander's troops. Hundreds of rebels were killed, and their bodies thrown into this cave.

Destroyed by John Hyrcanus, Samaria was magnificently rebuilt by Herod the Great and named Sebaste, or Augustus, in honour of the Roman emperor. Here he married lovely, ill-fated Mariamne, John Hyrcanus' great-great-granddaughter, and here, according to some sources, their two handsome sons, Alexander and Aristobolus, were murdered, victims of their father's insane jealousy of their popularity with the nation.

As the Herodian era drew to a close, Samaria became more and more a Roman city. Demobilized Roman soldiers were encouraged to settle there; the stadium in the valley, built by Herod, was enlarged; a pagan temple was added; and the ring road, with its pillared walks, put an extra touch of luxury to the amenities of this pleasant town.

With the adoption of Christianity as the official religion of the Roman Empire in AD 325, the heathen altars were gradually replaced by churches, but despite these changes, Samaria declined, while nearby Nablus grew. It is until today a flourishing town, the chief city of the entire area of Samaria.

Tulkarem, Tirza, Dothan, Jenin

Tulkarem, a thriving market town on the border between the Sharon Plain and the hills of Samaria, about 15 kilometres east of Netanya and 25 kilometres west of Nablus, has about 16,000 Arab inhabitants. Its best-known institution is the King Hussein College, originally the Agricultural School established in 1930 with funds provided by a wealthy Jew, Sir Ellis Kadoorie. Sir Ellis, an Iraqi Jew who lived in Hong Kong, bequeathed a large sum of money for the fostering of agricultural educa-

Scene near Ein Fara

tion in Palestine, not specifying whether it was to be for Jews or Arabs, so the British authorities divided the bequest into two, and set up one school for Arabs in Tulkarem, and another at Kfar Tabor, in Galilee.

Tirza, by the rich spring of Ein Farah, was for twenty years the capital of the kings of Israel. Set upon a hill, 10 kilometres north of Shechem and adjoining a fertile, well-watered valley, it was one of the Canaanite city-states conquered by Joshua. Jeroboam, king of Israel, made his first capital in Shechem, then moved it to Tirza, where it remained as the chief city of the Ten Tribes through the reigns of Baasha, Elah and Zimri. Then came a fight for the throne in which Omri, captain of the host, was victorious, and when Zimri saw he was defeated, he 'went into the palace of the king's house, and burnt it over him with fire, and died'. Omri remained in Tirza for six years, then bought the neighbouring hill of Samaria and erected his new capital there.

Once Omri moved his headquarters from Tirza to Samaria, the town declined, then was razed when the Assyrians conquered Samaria in 722 BC. Around 600 BC it was finally abandoned, and except for an odd building or two, so it has remained until the present day.

Nothing distinguishes the small Arab village of Tayasir, on a side road 3 kilometres north-west of Tubas except for the striking Roman mausoleum in its midst. A 2nd- or 3rd-century AD burial place of some wealthy Roman family, its colossal moulded, single-stone lintel, finely worked masonry and strange underground crypt are remarkably photogenic.

Haman el-Malik ('Hot Salt Baths') is the name given to a series of warm mineral springs gushing up from the wooded valley of Wadi Malik, some 7 kilometres past Tayasir towards the Jordan Valley. From a little distance it looks charming, for the palms thriving in the tepid, slightly brackish water and the lush vegetation give it a park-like air. At close quarters, however, the valley and the individual cabins, with the spring water flowing past, are dirty and neglected, and what could be one of the beauty spots of the country is painfully neglected. There are signs that these baths were extensively used in former times, and the Crusaders even built a castle there, not so much to guard the baths as to protect the mountain pass between the hills of Samaria and the Jordan Valley.

Dothan's ruins stand on a hill-top above a broad, lush Valley of Dothan, around 7 kilometres south-west of Jenin. Tradition identifies it with the biblical Dothan, where 'Joseph went after his brethren, and found them . . .' Envious of their father's special love for Joseph, his older brothers 'stripped Joseph out of his coat, his coat of many colours . . . and cast him into a pit', from where he was taken and sold as a slave.

Excavated by the American School of Oriental Research from 1953 to 1960, Dothan today shows evidence of having been a large and thriving city. Paved streets, gates, water cisterns and agricultural installations for preparing wine and olive oil and for grain storage indicated that Dothan was the granary for the surrounding countryside.

The protracted dig revealed signs of a Chalcolithic settlement of the fourth millennium BC, followed by an Early Bronze Age walled city from around 1700–1550, the era of the Hyksos. This layer showed that here was carried out the practice, common in those times, of burying infants in jars beneath the threshold of a building in order to placate the pagan gods.

In Joseph's day, Dothan was still a flourishing town, and it continued to be so during the period of the Judges and of the Kingdom of Israel, when it became the district centre. Remains of a multi-storied council house, store rooms and even a cellar with more than a hundred huge, intact storage jars for various products hint at the fullness of life in the Dothan of nearly three thousand years ago.

Dothan was burned to the ground by the Assyrians in 722 BC, when they conquered Samaria. The Assyrians themselves then erected a farming colony there, and rare Assyrian utensils – found in few places – were discovered on the spot. Except for two insignificant settlements, one from around the 3rd century AD and a comparatively recent Mameluke one, Dothan has since been deserted.

Strategically placed, Jenin, some 40 kilometres north of Nablus, is already mentioned as the town of Beit Hagan in documents of the second millennium BC. It was also the biblical city of Ein Ganim, then, as now, one of the major road junctions in the country. Not only was it a post on the 'Patriarchs' Way' from Aza to Damascus, but from it roads branched out to Afula, Nazareth and Galilee, to Acre and the sea, to Megiddo and to Tubas and the Jordan Valley.

Militarily important in Crusader times, too, it was then called La Grande Gerin to distinguish it from the nearby village of La Petite Gerin, now the abandoned hamlet of Zerin. Present-day Jenin is a small Arab town of some 16,000 people, still of military significance. During World War One it was a base for the combined Turkish-German forces, and later it became the main camp of the Iraqi troops poised to strike at Israel on the eve of the War of Independence. Actually, Israel's Army conquered all the villages around Jenin in June 1948, but was forced to abandon them with heavy losses. Nineteen years after, Jenin was taken by the Israelis.

Before you close this book please bear in mind that the places mentioned are only a fraction of those you can see around Jerusalem and in Judea and Samaria. Given time to explore, you will doubtless discover your own treasures, like the Monastery in the Wilderness close to Ein Karem; Khirbet Sa'adim, with its huge Greek-inscribed lintel near the Kennedy Memorial; or the spring at Lifta, just off the Tel Aviv–Jerusalem highway as it enters the capital.

Perhaps the memories you store away will not be of buildings or inanimate objects, but of the purple cyclamen and scarlet anemones scattered over the Judean Hills in springtime, or the flight of birds as they swoop across the semi-desert rolling down to the Dead Sea. Maybe you will recall even more vividly garlanded toddlers clutching baskets of fruit and flowers as they celebrate the Feast of Weeks, the festival of the early harvest; a group of school children setting out with saplings in their hands to plant a tree on traditional Tu B'shvat, or the participation in a *seder* meal shared with an Israeli family. Whatever your particular interest, in an area so steeped in history and presently such a lively population centre, you are likely to find it here.

Index

238

Sylvia Mann, London-born free-lance writer, studied opto-metry at London University. Here she met her seventh-generation *sabra* husband, then a medical student, and re-turned with him to Israel in 1949. Fascinated by the old-new land, the Manns and their four children (today either quali-fied or embryo physicians) began to explore the country, particularly the Jerusalem area. Sylvia's first piece, 'The Pools of Sataf', appeared in the *Jerusalem Post* in May 1963. Since then she has written innumerable articles; a book in Hebrew (*Atarei Yerushalaim*) and one in English (*Tour Jerusalem*), in addition to the present volume.

David Harris, free-lance photographer, was born in Jeru-salem in 1929. Interested in photography from the time he was a youngster attending Jerusalem's Ma'ale School, he later spent a year at the School of Modern Photography in New York, graduating with distinction. From 1948 to 1958 he was on the staff of the Jewish Agency's Publicity and Informa-tion Department; then he decided to strike out on his own and has been deservedly successful. Apart from his news pictures and participation in other works, he has illustrated a number of books, including *Nazareth, In the Footsteps of Jesus,* and *In the Footsteps of Moses.*